O9-ABE-489

Revolutionary America:

An Interpretive Overview

THE HARBRACE HISTORY OF THE UNITED STATES

Revolutionary America:
An Interpretive Overview

Robert M. Calhoon
University of North Carolina at Greensboro

Under the General Editorship of
John Morton Blum, Yale University

 HARCOURT BRACE JOVANOVICH, INC.

New York   Chicago   San Francisco   Atlanta

For my mother and father
and Peggy and Mary

Frontispiece: A German conception of "The
Destruction of the Royal Statue in New York" on
July 9, 1776. Etching, ca. 1776, engraved and published by François Xavier Habermann, Augsburg,
1776. Courtesy Library of Congress.

The excerpts (most of Chapter 1 and the
subsection in Chapter 2, "The Ideology of
Resistance") adapted from Chapters 2, 9, and 17 of
*The Loyalists in Revolutionary
America*, copyright © 1973, by
Robert M. Calhoon, are reprinted by permission of
Harcourt Brace Jovanovich, Inc.

Page 171: Adapted from *The National Experience:
A History of the United States* by John. M. Blum
et al., p. 121. © 1963 Harcourt Brace Jovanovich.

© 1976 by Harcourt Brace Jovanovich, Inc.

All rights reserved. No part of this publication
may be reproduced or transmitted in any form or
by any means, electronic or mechanical, including
photocopy, recording, or any information storage
and retrieval system, without permission in
writing from the publisher.

ISBN: 0-15-576712-7

Library of Congress Catalog Card Number: 75-32465

Printed in the United States of America

*Page 204 constitutes a continuation of the copy-
right page.*

Preface

Revolutionary America is a survey of the significant events and the most recent historical interpretations of the Revolutionary period. As the title indicates, my aim is to go beyond the main events that are generally accepted as comprising the American Revolution: the rebellion that erupted in the thirteen colonies in 1774–1775; the Americans' declaration of their independence in 1776; and the war waged for seven years in defense of that independence. In addition to describing those events *Revolutionary America* discusses the successive crises in colonial-imperial relations between 1764 and 1774 that precipitated the rebellion, as well as the underlying stresses in the British Empire that exhibited themselves as early as the 1750s. It also examines the burst of constitution-writing that began in the states in 1776 and continued through the drafting and ratification of the Federal Constitution of 1787.

Yet even this bare outline of events raises a host of questions:

Why, despite the fact that the Empire was based on an intelligent and workable set of institutions, did such strong antagonisms develop between the colonies and Great Britain? Why did British officials and colonial leaders find each other's concepts and arguments incomprehensible?

What fears, hopes, ideas, and aspirations motivated the colonists to resist British authority between 1765 and 1776? What did ideology mean to the colonists, and how did it transform the experience of an otherwise hardheaded, realistic people? What tactics did colonial resisters use?

What was the impact of the War for Independence on American

society? What were the sources of division, violence, and strife in the colonies, and how well were they exploited by British generals and their loyalist supporters? How did the dislocations of war, inflation, black participation in the resistance, and internal subversion change American society?

Why was the drafting and implementation of written constitutions the central task and the greatest achievement of the Revolutionary era? How did the constitution-makers view human nature and the possibilities of republican government? How did constitution-making become a search for stable, legitimate authority?

This book shows how historians have tried to answer these questions and, more importantly, how they have sharpened and reshaped the questions themselves as research and writing on the Revolution intensified during the past decade. By examining recent studies on slavery, religion, urban discontent, violence, and economic dislocation, as well as the more familiar subject areas of colonial grievances, political ideas, and constitutional innovations, *Revolutionary America* seeks to tap and communicate the immense vitality of Revolutionary scholarship.

Like any interrogation, the questions one asks the historical record reflect certain prior assumptions, hunches, and points of view. My own approach and bias should be stated at the outset.

The Revolution was more than a national movement for justice, freedom, and dignity. The colonies were a developing society in the 1760s and early 1770s; the flaws and contradictions in the character of the people both speeded up and retarded the movement of resistance to external authority. The colonists had an insatiable appetite for British credit, investment, and consumer goods. The resulting materialism and chronic debt both conflicted with and heightened their desire to be a Spartan society with a more equitable distribution of wealth and opportunity than could be found in the Old World. Much of their economic abundance and widespread opportunity depended on the institution of slavery. Anxious to compensate for this flaw in their moral order and fearful of slave uprisings and even divine retribution, slave-owning colonists strove with special diligence to conduct their political affairs wisely and prudently. The planter aristocracy in the southern colonies was one of the most unified segments of society supporting resistance and independence.

Most significantly, the colonists lacked an authoritative culture— that is, a widely practiced, integrated set of ideas about how people ought to behave. When they looked for models of a good society, they turned to the heroic efforts of the early settlers or to the cosmopolitan brilliance of contemporary London. A close look at their own leading towns, however, suggested that the evils of London—poverty and violence, turbulent radical politics, press gangs brutally commandeering seamen for service in the British navy, and alarming displays of material ostentation—had already begun to infect urban America.

As a subordinate, dependent people, the colonists became fascinated, even obsessed, with the nature of political power. As British officials and institutions seemed increasingly to abuse their authority, the colonists concluded that ultimate political power—the last line of defense against tyranny—should be lodged in a place secure from human greed and corruption: the whole body of the people. It was a daring and not completely successful innovation. Americans continue to cope with the immense burdens imposed on those who live in a democratic society in which government is answerable to the people, and the people answerable to each other and to future generations for their faithful stewardship of that trust.

This book is an outgrowth of my earlier study *The Loyalists in Revolutionary America, 1760–1781* (Harcourt Brace Jovanovich, 1973). Most of Chapter 1 and the subsection in Chapter 2 on "The Ideology of Resistance" are adapted from Chapters 2, 9, and 17 of that book. I am grateful to William B. Goodman for his encouragement in the preparation of both these books and to that Company for its permission to use the material from one in the other.

The study of early American history—as Robert Zemsky observes —can today be practically a "public enterprise," so generous and collegial are one's fellow workers in this field. John Morton Blum, John M. Murrin, and Gary B. Nash each gave the manuscript a most searching and constructive critique. Michael O'Doherty did the same for Chapter 3. Jack P. Greene has given generously of his time, interest, and insight to my work, and his writings have in large part defined the issues facing early American historians. Conversations with Murray Arndt, David V. J. Bell, Converse D. Clowse, Ira Gruber, Don Higginbotham, Donald G. Mathews, Mary Beth Norton, Loren Schweninger, Paul H. Smith, and Robert M. Weir have helped me think through and clarify my understanding of the Revolutionary era. At the University of North Carolina at Greensboro, I am grateful to Richard Bardolph, Warren Ashby, Dean Robert L. Miller, Vice Chancellor Stanley L. Jones, Chancellor James S. Ferguson, and James H. Thompson, for their support; and to students in the History Department and Residential College for their discoveries and enthusiasm, especially Ellen Deitz, Susan Greninger, James Heilman, Martha Hyatt, Brenda Massingale, Annette Cox Smith, Rick Stone, David Turner, and Denise Walston.

Audiences at Florida Technological University, the Air Force Academy, the University of California at Irvine, the Institute of United States Studies at the University of London, and the University of East Anglia listened to portions of the book and raised helpful questions; and I am grateful to my hosts on those occasions: Samuel Proctor, Jerrill Shofner, Alfred F. Hurley, Keith L. Nelson, Esmond Wright, and Howard Temperley.

William J. Wisneski, Elizabeth Holland, and Abigail Winograd edited the manuscript with care and intelligence, and Yvonne Steiner selected the excellent illustrations.

Most of the facts and much of the interpretation in the book derive from the work of the scholars listed in the notes and bibliographies. Though it is an imperfect rendering of their work, my debt and appreciation to them is beyond calculation.

Doris and Marie Calhoon have made the effort worthwhile.

ROBERT M. CALHOON

Contents

4   Constitutionalism   161

Revolutionary America:

An Interpretive Overview

Empire 1

The Americans have made a discovery, or
think they have made one, that we mean to
oppress them; we have made a discovery, or
think we have made one, that they intend to
rise in rebellion. We do not know how to advance; they do not know how to retreat. *

Edmund Burke to the House of Commons,
1769

THE GROWTH OF THE BRITISH EMPIRE

At the start of the seventeenth century England had no settled
overseas colonies. Less than one and three quarters of a century
later—at the close of the Seven Years' War in 1763—England had
become the center of a vast and powerful domain. The British[1] Empire included the eastern half of the North American continent, a
dozen rich sugar-producing islands in the West Indies, slave-trading
outposts in Africa, and extensive commercial influence in
India—to mention only the most important fruits of British expansion. That remarkable achievement in imperial growth occurred in

* Quoted in Michael Kammen, *Rope of Sand* (Ithaca: Cornell University Press,
1968), p. 167.

1 A contemporary view of Elizabethan overseas expansion—"A Hieroglyphic of Britain" from John Dee, *Arte of Navigation* (1577).

North America in several distinct stages. First, between 1607 and 1638 religious groups and investment companies secured charters from the Crown for the establishment of seven colonies in the Chesapeake and New England regions, among them Virginia, founded in 1607; Plymouth, in 1620; Massachusetts Bay, in 1629; Maryland, in 1634; Connecticut, in 1635; and Rhode Island, in

1636. Cut off from direct English control and left almost completely alone during the English Civil War and Cromwellian dictatorship in the 1640s and 1650s, the new colonies struggled to establish a viable agricultural and commercial economy and to adapt to the rigors of the wilderness.

Next, during the 1620s and 1630s English emigrants settled islands in the Caribbean—Barbados, Nevis, Monsarrat, St. Christopher, and Antigua, and later Jamaica, following its seizure from Spain in 1655. During the remainder of the seventeenth century the planter class on these sugar-producing islands became enormously rich by exploiting the lush growing conditions and using massive amounts of slave labor. But hurricanes, disease, humidity, violence, and a debauched life-style proved the ruination of many of these settlers.

2 Perils of the earliest colonial settlements in the American wilderness.

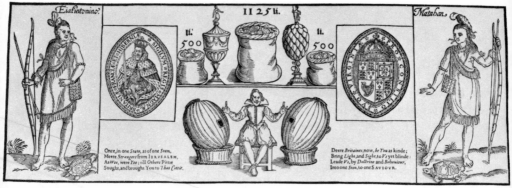

3 Advertisement for a lottery in England to raise funds in support of the Virginia colony showing lottery tickets and amounts of the prizes.

Then with the restoration of Charles II in 1660 came a new period of colonial expansion on the North American mainland. Between the mid-1660s and early 1680s a new breed of ambitious colonial organizers secured land grants and charters for colonies in New York, New Jersey, Carolina, Pennsylvania, and Delaware. The economic success of these colonies depended on a high level of immigration and rapid distribution of land. By promising cheap land, low taxes, religious toleration, and representative government, the new colonial proprietors further contributed to a social and politi-

4 New York harbor in 1757 by an unknown artist.

cal order characterized by weak political authority and unrestrained individual enterprise.

Finally, Britain's long struggle with France and Spain for commercial and colonial supremacy resulted in a further enlargement of the Empire. In the Peace of Utrecht in 1713 Britain gained Newfoundland, Nova Scotia, and a monopoly of the Atlantic slave trade. By the Peace of Paris in 1763, which ended the Seven Years' War (called the French and Indian War in America), France ceded all of its North American possessions east of the Mississippi and Spain surrendered Florida. The cost of defending and administering the new territories, as well as the enormous debt accumulated during the Seven Years' War, forced Britain to impose on the colonies the taxes and commercial restrictions that were a major cause of the American Revolution.

Throughout this process Britain and the colonies affected each other in a variety of ways. The colonies became an outlet for the thousands of restless, daring, dissatisfied men and women thrust up by uncertain economic and political conditions in sixteenth- and seventeenth-century England. Colonies also provided a refuge for persecuted religious sects—Puritans in New England, Quakers in Pennsylvania, Catholics in Maryland. As England became a

more stable, militarily powerful, and modern society between the 1670s and 1720s, its government increasingly became a bureaucracy, and the administration of the Empire fell to impersonal government agencies. As the colonies prospered and matured during the eighteenth century, colonists tended to imitate English culture and at the same time to resent and resist imperial centralization and control.

The Empire flourished during the eighteenth century in large part because the colonies had an expanding market economy and a burgeoning population. Between 1700 and 1750 colonial imports from Britain grew 450 percent, and from 1697 to 1775 colonial exports to the mother country increased sevenfold. In 1700 the mainland colonies had a population of 200,000; by 1763 this number had risen to 2,000,000; to 2,500,000 by 1776; and to nearly 4,000,000 by the ratification of the Constitution in 1788. The urban population of the colonies increased sharply during the late colonial period; by 1775 Philadelphia had a population of 40,000; New York, 25,000; Boston, 16,000; and Charles Town, 12,000. In every colony there were networks of trade and communication, formed by secondary ports like Portsmouth, New Hampshire; Wilmington, North Carolina; and Savannah, Georgia; and by inland trading centers like Hartford, Connecticut; Albany, New York; Cross Creek, North Carolina; Camden, South Carolina; and Augusta, Georgia.

5 Baltimore, Maryland, as a small agricultural and fishing settlement in 1752.

With a population of just under 690,000 the New England states were overcrowded—in terms of a pre-industrial, largely agrarian society—by the time of the Revolution. Agriculture was centered in river valleys, and the population clustered in towns whose boundaries extended several miles into the countryside. Half of the population of the middle colonies—300,000 out of a total of 600,000—lived in Pennsylvania, where waves of German-speaking and then Scots-Irish settlers had come during the colonial period. Thousands of settlers from these two groups moved down through the Shenandoah Valley of Virginia into the Piedmont frontier of the Carolinas and Georgia. New York, with its emphasis on tenant farming on the great estates of the Hudson Valley, was less attractive to emigrants. The tidewater and coastal southern colonies had a population of more than a million people in 1775, nearly half of whom were slaves. Although the southern colonies had a substantial yeoman farmer class, the planter aristocracy from Maryland to Georgia dominated the society.

At every stage in the growth of the Empire and in Britain's emergence as an imperial power, a single common assumption underlay colonial policy: colonies existed to enhance the power and wealth of the mother country. Mercantilism was a set of rules based on that assumption and implemented in a series of statutes passed by Parliament between 1650 and 1764.

7

6 Chesapeake-region planters engaged in a fox hunt.

The most important of these laws were the Navigation Act of 1660, which established a commercial system at the time of the restoration of Charles II; the Navigation Act of 1696, which revamped the system under a powerful Board of Trade; and the Sugar Act of 1764, which tightened enforcement of the acts of trade. These laws required that trade within the Empire be conducted in English or colonial ships manned by English or colonial crews. At the heart of the Navigation Acts was the practice of "enumeration": the listing of commodities that could be shipped only within the Empire—tobacco, rice, naval stores (tar, pitch, and ship rigging), and indigo. The acts of trade relegated the colonies to a role of supplier of raw materials for Britain and market for finished British products. In order to stimulate colonial production of staples and encourage colonial consumption of British exports, the system made numerous concessions to colonial interests. Cash bounties were paid to the producers of naval stores. The English were forbidden to raise tobacco in order to protect Virginia from crippling competition. To rescue South Carolina from chronic economic depression, in 1730 the British permitted Charles Town merchants to

❧ By the King.

¶ A Proclamation for the vtter prohibiting the importation and vſe of all Tobacco, which is not of the proper growth of the Colonies of *Virginia* and the *Summer Ijlands*, or one of them.

Hereas, at the humble ſuite of Our Commons in Parliament, by Our Royall Proclamation, bearing date the nine and twentieth day of September now laſt paſt, for the reaſons therein contained, wee haue prohibited the importation and vſe of all Tobacco, which is not of the proper growth of Our Colonies of Virginia and the Summer Iſlands, or one of them; And whereas, vpon the humble petition of many Our louing Subiects, being Planters or Aduenturers in thoſe Colonies, and for the ſupport and incouragement of thoſe Plantations (whoſe proſperous eſtate wee much affect, and ſhall by all good meanes be alwayes ready to cheriſh and protect) wee haue beene contented to tolerate the vſe of Tobacco, of the growth of thoſe Plantations for a time, vntill by more ſolid Commodities they be able to ſubſiſt otherwiſe, which (as wee are informed) they cannot as yet by any meanes doe: And therefore by Our ſaid Proclamation, wee did thinke fit to giue particular directions in many things tending to thoſe ends, and did ſtraitly command the due execution and obſeruation thereof, vnder the penalties therein contained: Now becauſe wee haue beene informed, aſwell by the humble Certificate of Our Commiſſioners for Virginia, as by the humble petition of diuers of Our louing Subiects, the Planters and Aduenturers of, and in thoſe Colonies, That, notwithſtanding Our Royall pleaſure was ſo expreſſely ſignified, and the reaſons of State are ſo plainely laid downe, as might haue perſwaded euery well affected Subiect to the due obſeruance thereof; yet diuers, out of an inordinate deſire of priuate gaine, haue wilfully diſobeyed Our commandement herein, and thereby haue indeauoured, as much as in them lieth, to deſtroy ſo noble a worke as the ſupport of thoſe Plantations, which ſo much concernes Our Honour, and the honour and profit of Our people.

Wee therefore, being very ſenſible of this neglect and contempt, haue thought good to renew Our ſaid Proclamation; And doe hereby ſignifie and declare vnto all Our louing Subiects, and vnto all others, Our expreſſe will and pleaſure to be, That Our ſaid former Proclamation, and euery clauſe, prohibition, article and thing therein contained, ſhall from henceſoorth be duly obſerued and obeyed. With ſuch alterations and additions, as are in theſe preſents contained and expreſſed, vpon paine of Our high diſpleaſure, and ſuch penalties and puniſhments, as in Our ſaid former Proclamation are, or in theſe preſents ſhall be limited or appointed for the offenders thereof.

And whereas ſome haue ſince Our ſaid laſt Proclamation, vnmerchantliſe, ſecretly and cunningly ſtollen in great parcels of Tobacco, contrary to Our ſaid Proclamation; wee would haue thoſe perſons, and all others by their example know, That they muſt expect the ſeueritie of that cenſure, which Our Court of Starre-Chamber ſhall thinke fit to inflict vpon them, and that wee are reſolued not to relent or remit their deſerued puniſhment, but to cauſe them and all others, that ſhall dare to offend herein, to bee proſecuted and puniſhed in ſuch meaſure, as ſuch their high contempt doth deſerue.

And becauſe wee conceiued it would be vtterly in baine to prohibite the importation of ſuch forreine Tobacco, as aforeſaid, vnleſſe the care and charge of the execution thereof were committed by Us, to ſome fit and able perſons, who beſides the reſpect to Our ſeruice, might for their owne particular intereſts take the ſame to heart; Therefore wee haue by Our Letters Patents vnder Our great Seale

---

7   Royal Proclamation in 1624 giving Virginia and Bermuda exclusive control of the export of tobacco to England (Bermuda was at this time known as the Summer Islands).

ship their rice crop directly to the Iberian peninsula rather than sell it through British middlemen as strict mercantilist practice required.

Mercantilism worked to the benefit of both the colonies and Britain, not only because of concessions to colonial interests, but also because the capricious and rigid features of the system simply proved to be unenforceable. As a reward to the West Indian planters for the wealth that the sugar trade brought to Britain, Parliament passed in 1733 the Molasses Act, placing a prohibitive duty on the cheaper and better-grade French molasses imported by New England merchants for distillation into rum. By widespread smuggling of French molasses, however, the New England merchants maintained profitable commerce with the French West Indies. Moreover, British law forbade the export of gold or silver coin to the colonies, prohibited the colonists from minting coins, and only occasionally sanctioned the printing of paper money. The need for a larger and

8   Quaker sugar planters in Barbados in the 1690s.

more responsive money supply increased the amount of illicit trade between the mainland colonies and the French, Spanish, and Dutch West Indies. This commerce not only brought gold into the colonial money supply; the higher profits from illegal trade in the Caribbean provided colonial merchants with investment capital needed for expansion of their legitimate trade within the Empire. In addition, the British customs service lacked the manpower and expertise to check enumerated cargoes closely, and only a fraction of the export duties on legitimate trade was ever collected. Lax enforcement, however, actually stimulated imperial commerce. Truly stringent checking of papers and searches of cargoes would have seriously hampered the speed and volume of trade. Colonial merchants apparently only violated the acts of trade systematically when there was some overriding economic necessity to do so. The impracticality of enforcing restrictive mercantilist regulations had, therefore, a salutary effect on the economy of the whole Empire.

THE STRUCTURE OF COLONIAL SUBORDINATION

Just as mercantilism was a contradictory mixture of inducements and prohibitions, so the political structure of the Empire was an amalgam of liberties and controls. There were four major links between the colonies and Britain: the royal governments, a trans-Atlantic network of political allies, the money supply, and the various executive agencies of the British government that dealt with colonial policy. The first and most important set of political bonds connecting the thirteen North American colonies to the mother country were the royal governments, which replaced decrepit charter and proprietary administrations. In Virginia a royal government was set up in 1624; in New York, after its proprietor, the Duke of York, became king in 1685; in New Hampshire, after its separation from Massachusetts in 1679; in Massachusetts in 1691; in Maryland from 1689 to 1715; in New Jersey in 1701; in South Carolina in 1719; in North Carolina in 1729; and in Georgia in 1752. Royal governments brought continuity, a uniform constitution, and badly needed executive leadership to these colonies. Such governments were ostensibly based on the English unwritten

11

constitution, with its essential elements of King, Lords, and Commons. The governor was appointed by and represented the king, and the Crown supervised his performance with a detailed "Commission" outlining his powers and lengthy "Royal Instructions" specifying how he should deal with particular problems. His most important duties were summoning, dissolving, and proroguing (recessing) the assembly, approving or vetoing its legislation, and referring the legislation he signed to the Privy Council in London for further review. The lower, or popularly elected, house of the assembly served the functions of the English House of Commons; the royally appointed council was roughly the equivalent of the House of Lords. It shared legislative power with the lower house, though in practice it could not initiate or modify taxation or appropriation bills. The council also served as a local version of the Privy Council, officially advising the governor and being a party to some executive decisions. The most notable departure from this constitution scheme was the Massachusetts Charter of 1691, which allowed the legislature to elect—subject only to the governor's veto—the members of the council. Although the Massachusetts house tended to choose, and the governor to approve, councillors relatively sympathetic to the policies of the Crown, the Massachusetts council was an independent body that after 1765 increasingly sided with the popularly elected house against the governor.

At its best, royal government gave order and form to the still fragile and unstable colonial society; it brought security and predictability to the task of taming the wilderness and maintaining European standards of civility in a crude, unpolished social setting; it induced colonial leaders to put aside internecine faction strife and cooperate with the governor in promoting the colony's prosperity. William Gooch, Governor of Virginia from 1727 to 1749, persuaded the House of Burgesses to institute a far-reaching program to improve the market value of tobacco through a system of inspection and the destruction of low-quality leaves. He won local support for these reforms by making the inspection fair, honest, and impartial. He overcame opposition from the customs service,

9 Slaves in Virginia curing and treating tobacco.

which feared that export limitations on tobacco would reduce customs, the value of duties on tobacco, and thereby lower its income. In Massachusetts, Governor William Shirley (1741–1757) succeeded where his predecessors had failed in securing the cooperation of all the major factions in the colony. He engineered this political harmony by first persuading the assembly to support expensive military operations against the French in King George's War (1741–1748) and then bestowing the contracts, commissions, and civil offices that the war created on a wide circle of able colonial leaders.

Benning Wentworth, Governor of New Hampshire from 1741 to 1767, brought such benevolent, stabilizing techniques to the level of an art form. He acquired extensive power and wealth by con-

13

10 Governor William Shirley of Massachusetts.

structing a network of influences and alliances within New Hampshire itself, in neighboring Massachusetts, and in London. Through John Thomlinson, Wentworth's close associate in London, he secured the governorship and also the influential post of Surveyor of His Majesty's Forests in North America, an office that regulated lumbering and insured that the British navy would have a regular supply of masts, spars, and other shipbuilding necessities. Wentworth's numerous relatives dominated lumber, which was New Hampshire's chief export trade; and Thomlinson also secured for Wentworth and other New Hampshire merchants lucrative contracts to supply lumber for the navy. As governor, Wentworth could create new townships and grant the choice land in these locations to his political supporters. Intermarriage with a few prominent merchant families in Portsmouth made the Wentworths leaders of an aristocracy whose wealth was derived from lumbering, officeholding, land speculation, and commerce. Wentworth's judicious use of patronage and land grants and his lax enforcement of restrictions on lumbering placed the great majority of landowners and merchants of New Hampshire in his debt. The assembly therefore worked closely with the governor and relied on Wentworth's contacts in London to promote the colony's interest. A concentration of power, influence, and effectiveness in the Wentworth family gave New Hampshire a stable and prosperous political and social order.

Gooch, Shirley, and Wentworth brought royal government in America to its most effective level of performance; each man possessed leadership talents that fostered the economic expansion of his colony and enlarged the power and wealth of his colony's social elite. But the political institutions that benefited most from prosperity and the growth of aristocracy were the lower houses of assembly. Created during the earliest years of each colony's existence, the assemblies gave power and responsibility to the leading men of the colony who served as members. By the middle of the eighteenth century each of the assemblies had acquired exclusive power to initiate its colony's tax bills and audit its financial records, often the authority to supervise expenditures, and on occasion the power to print paper money. The lower houses acquired extensive control over militia, local government, public works, and Indian affairs. Control of the purse and the responsibility for paying salaries to many Crown officials, however, did not give the assemblies enough leverage to dictate to their governors. But the assemblies could bring specific operations of government to a halt by delaying the payment of a salary, refusing to build a needed fort, or failing to raise and arm militia in time of war. Lengthy debates about the conduct of particular Crown officials or protracted disputes between the lower house and the council could prevent the passage of needed routine legislation and embarrass the governor more than they inconvenienced the public. By steadily enlarging their control over finance and policy and scrutinizing every action of Crown officials, the assemblies transformed American politics during the half-century from 1713 to 1763.

The assemblies succeeded partly because they proved to be far

15

more adaptable political institutions than the agencies of the Crown. During the seventeenth century, property qualifications for voting restricted the electorate to a quarter of the adult white male population; however, the growing availability of land after 1713 enlarged the electorate so that by the 1760s probably 95 percent of adult white males could vote in Massachusetts, perhaps 75 percent in New York and Virginia. Candidates for the assemblies were almost always men of property and standing in the colony. Men of humbler station lacked the time, training, and incentive to hold office, and by tradition the bulk of the population deferred to members of the elite. Political contests, then, pitted rival segments of the aristocracy against each other. To win an election a candidate needed both the backing of powerful political sponsors and the approval of the voters. Oratorical eloquence, a reputation for honesty or shrewdness or piety or business acumen, and a respected family name were among the qualities that voters favored. Within the assembly a further screening of talent occurred. Through an elaborate committee system a core of experienced and hardworking legislators monopolized the power of the assembly. These were the men who did the tedious work of responding line by line to governors' messages; in the process they learned how to distinguish their own ideas about public policy from those propounded by Crown officials and royal governors. The exchange of messages between governors and assemblies forced assemblymen constantly to refurbish and refine the idea that the colonies had a contractual relationship with the mother country—a contract that guaranteed the preservation of representative government and individual liberty. Unintentionally the Crown encouraged the assemblies to think of themselves as bulwarks of liberty, miniature parliaments designed to check and counteract any excessive use of prerogative power by the Crown. Royal instructions to governors cautioned that lower houses were not to exercise "any power or privilege . . . which is not allowed . . . the House of Commons . . . in Great Britain."[2] This comparison was a heady stimulant to colonial politics, for the image that eighteenth-century Americans had of the House of Commons came from the seventeenth century, when the Commons had resisted and whittled down the prerogative power of the Stuart monarchy. At the very least, the tendency to imitate the House of Commons brought regularity and a sense of seriousness to colonial politics.

Despite the apparent maturity and vitality of political institutions in America, the constitution of the Empire—as it applied to the colonies—was fundamentally unstable. Difficult to diagnose and impossible to correct at the time, this instability derived from the fact that the executive branches of the governments in the royal colonies—governors, councils, and other appointed officials—possessed far more formal power than they did informal political influence and leverage. The governor of a royal colony could summon, prorogue, or dissolve its assembly at will, while in Britain a new Parliamentary election had to be called every seven years and Parliament effectively controlled the duration of its sessions. Governors frequently thwarted hostile resolutions by proroguing assemblies without warning and extending the recesses for long periods of time. The governor had an absolute veto over all colonial laws, and the Privy Council often disallowed laws that the governor allowed to stand; British kings in the eighteenth century had tacitly relinquished authority to disapprove acts passed by Parliament, but royal governors used the veto regularly. Finally, the Crown claimed the power to dismiss royally appointed colonial judges at will, although British judges could be removed only for proven misconduct. In contrast with these formal powers, which exceeded those of the Crown in Great Britain, royal officials in America lacked the informal power that enabled the British government at home to get things done. The governors—except in New Hampshire and to a lesser extent in Massachusetts—had little patronage to dispense. Royal councils were intended to provide the governor with a group of wealthy and prestigious advisers who shared with him the responsibility for maintaining British authority; but for a variety of reasons the councils steadily declined in prestige and power and were often more of an embarrassment than a support for the governor. Consequently, many governors felt a galling sense of impotence. On the one hand, the governors' 17 extensive formal powers aroused deep apprehension and kept the assemblies in a state of defensiveness, while, on the other, the governors' lack of informal influence weakened their capacity to deal firmly and fairly with the assemblies.

None of these restrictions existed in the two charter colonies, Connecticut and Rhode Island. Apart from owing allegiance to the king and being obliged to obey the Navigation Acts, these two colonies were virtually autonomous. Voters in both colonies elected the assembly, council, and governor. As in Massachusetts, however, real political power rested in the towns, where it was shared by prominent families and the mass of the populace, and neither side was powerful enough to ride roughshod over the other. Moreover, in both colonies a two-party factional system developed; and while electioneering was often fierce and bitter, each faction was effectively checked by its rival.

Because the proprietor occupied a position analogous to that of the Crown, politics in the proprietary colonies of Pennsylvania, Delaware, and Maryland more nearly resembled the pattern of the royal colonies. Pennsylvania politics were extremely complex. The Penn family owned vast estates and used its control of the governorship to preserve its tax privileges and thwart the ambitions of the Quaker aristocracy in Philadelphia. A large number of German-speaking settlers tended to vote as a bloc for whichever party would protect their interests. Three parties, at one time or another, contended for power. The pacifist Quaker aristocracy dominated the assembly until 1757, when most of its leaders withdrew from politics rather than vote public funds as bounties for Indian scalps during the Seven Years' War. Then a party led by Benjamin Franklin and a lawyer named Joseph Galloway came to the fore as the enemy of the privileges of the Penn family. In 1764 the Franklin-Galloway majority in the assembly even voted to ask Britain to make Pennsylvania a royal colony—although nothing came of the application. From 1766 to 1774 Galloway assumed the role of apologist for British policy. A third party, led by John Dickinson, also a lawyer, had consistently opposed the Franklin-Galloway group; from 1765 onward it organized resistance in Pennsylvania to

11 Quaker settlers in
Pennsylvania befriending
the Indians.

British encroachments. Delaware was also a possession of the
Penns, but it had little organized political life until independence.
In Maryland successive Lords Baltimore, residing in England, kept
a tight hold over the colony through the appointment of able, loyal
proprietary officials. Gradually the assembly became dominated by
antiproprietary politicians whose antipathy to executive power resembled that of assemblymen in royal colonies.

The anxiety with which governors and colonial politicians eyed
each others' powers prompted both groups to stabilize colonial politics by establishing a network of relationships with highly placed
political patrons in England. Most Crown officials and many colonial politicians depended on allies within the ruling circles in
London to intervene with Parliament or agencies of the Crown in a
host of mundane matters—appointments, minor changes in the   19

acts of trade, legal decisions of colonial courts that had been appealed to the Privy Council. Thus Benning Wentworth had John Thomlinson; William Gooch had close ties with key political advisers of Robert Walpole, who was head of the ministry; James De Lancey, the most powerful politician in New York during the 1740s and 1750s, owed his position to a network of high-ranking allies in London, including the Archbishop of Canterbury. This system of personal trans-Atlantic ties worked well during the first half of the eighteenth century because Parliament was dominated by an extensive alliance of Whig factions and the responsibility for colonial policy was fragmented. The work of governing the colonies was mainly a matter of competition over patronage: the distribution of royal offices in America to deserving supporters of the various factional leaders in British politics. In this situation highly placed allies of governors and colonial leaders could influence patronage decisions and obstruct efforts by executive agencies of the imperial bureaucracy to impose coercive controls on the colonies.

Throughout the 1730s and 1740s the distribution of government jobs in the colonies was in the hands of the Duke of Newcastle, the great patronage broker of the period. Control of these appointments kept Newcastle and his friends in power. That political stability, in turn, enabled the government to concentrate on expanding trade, keeping taxes low, and promoting prosperity. But in the 1750s the system began to come apart. The great coalition of factions led by Newcastle began to fragment into squabbling factions. At the same time, many of the English contacts for colonial politicians grew old and passed from the scene. Politics became more competitive and acrimonious, and patronage could no longer calm political conflicts as it had in the past.

The Seven Years' War, with its high taxes for landowners and high profits for merchants, created fresh political discord. In order to win the war, Newcastle had to share leadership of the government with an aggressive war minister, William Pitt. Pitt instructed colonial governors to make almost any concessions in order to secure the wholehearted support of the colonial assemblies for the war effort. This policy helped defeat the French, but it also gave the assemblies a sudden increase in power and autonomy. Therefore, colonial politicians in the assemblies, after 1760, no longer felt that they needed the help of highly placed contacts in England. At this very time, those contacts were losing their ability to deliver favors and influence for colonial clients. War, moreover, created vast new wealth for British merchants, and the scramble to share this booty weakened the old London merchant houses and joint stock companies and strengthened newly emerged merchant firms in Bristol, Liverpool, and Glasgow. Too, the mercantile interest groups that lobbied Parliament and the ministry became smaller, more specialized, and more numerous than the interest groups of the early eighteenth century.

Given the central role of trade in the life of the Empire and eco-

12   A colonial merchant's counting house.

COINS	Weights			Value	Lawfull Money	Silver Coins	Weights			Value	
	oz.	dw	gr	OLD TENOR £	s		oz.	dw	gr	£ s	
Guinea	0	5	9	10.10	28/-	Eng Crown	0	19	8½	2.10	
Half D.		2	16½	5.5	14/-	Half Ditto		9	16¼	1.5	
Moidore		6	22¼	13.10	36/-	Dollar		17	12	2.5	
Half D.		3	11	6.15	18/-	Half Ditto		8	18	1.2.6	
Dubloon or 4 Pistole Piece		17	8	33..	88/-	Quarter D.		4	9	.11.3	
Half D.		8	16	16.10	44/-						
Pistole		4	8	8.5	22/-						
Half D.		2	4	4.2.6	11/-						
Double Joannes or £3.12/ Sterl Piece		18	10	36..	96/-						
Single Joannas or 36/ Sterl Piece		9	5	18..	48/-						
Half D.		4	14½	9..	24/-						
Quarter D.		2	7¼	4.10	12/-						

			GOLD p. oz	SILVER p. oz
oz.	dw	gr		
1	0	0	£38.0.0	2.10.0
	10	0	19..	1.5..
	5	0	9.10	12.6
	2	0	3.16	.5..
	1	0	1.18	2.6
	0	12	19..	1.3
	0	6	9.6	0.7½
	0	3	4.9	0.3¾
	0	1	1.7	0.1¼

ENGRAV'D Printed & Sold by NAT HURD.

NB 24 Grains is one penny
nt 20 Penny wt one Ounce

13   A conversion table for various European coins circulating in the colonial economy.

nomic regulation in British administration of the colonies, the next critical link between Britain and the colonies was the money supply with which people in distant parts of the Empire paid each other for goods and services. The visible money supply took a number of forms: sterling notes, gold and silver coins, paper money issued by the individual colonies, and bills of exchange written by colonial merchants and chargeable to their sterling accounts in London. There was also an invisible money supply consisting of debts owed to British merchants and credit extended by those mer-

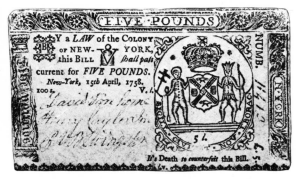

14a   Colonial paper currency.

23

14b · Colonial paper currency.

chants to colonial importers. Had the colonies and Britain been economic equals, these various forms of money would have been only functional tools of trade. But the colonies were economic subordinates of the mother country and could only respond to economic conditions that originated in Britain. The most important of those conditions was an enormous expansion of British economic activity between 1745 and 1775. During this period British merchants greatly increased their exports to the colonies by developing new methods of money management and by expanding credit they could extend to colonial importers. As long as the colonial staple products, like tobacco, rose in price, the colonial economy could support this widening gap between the value of British imports and colonial exports. But when these prices declined during periodic downturns in the economy of the Empire, the cost to colonists of paying sterling debts in London rose sharply. Locked into a position as a debtor to British creditors, overextended colonial merchants faced bankruptcy—especially during the severe colonial recession of 1764. Debts and credit were, therefore, both the life-blood of imperial trade and a source of harrowing tension and uncertainty for colonial businessmen.

During this period of flux in the political and economic life of the Empire, George II died, and in 1760 his young grandson as-

24

15   This print by William Hogarth defends the unpopular ministry of Lord Bute in 1762. The fire is the Seven Years' War. The man with the bellows is William Pitt, former prime minister and vehement critic of peace negotiations. The King or his representative (with GR armband) mans the hose.

cended to the throne as George III. Politically inexperienced but determined not to be manipulated by powerful factions, the new king quickly humiliated Newcastle, First Lord of the Treasury, by offering jobs and influence to opportunists among the Duke's Parliamentary backers; and if they continued to remain loyal to Newcastle, they were then purged from the government payroll. In so doing, George III and his adviser, the Earl of Bute, broke the power of the alliance of Whig factions that had governed Britain since 1713. Despite this initial success it would take the young king ten years to find a ministry that he could wholeheartedly support and that could command a dependable majority in the House of Commons. Into this power vacuum moved ministers such as George Grenville, Charles Townshend, and the Earl of Hills-

25

borough, who felt that political survival, let alone success, required that they finally impose order and system on the administration of the Empire. These men had close ties with the professionals in the imperial bureaucracy. Agencies of the Crown, such as the Privy Council, the Board of Trade, and the Treasury, had tried ever since 1696 to govern the Empire firmly, but they had always lacked sufficient Parliamentary or ministerial backing. Long thwarted and now suddenly successful in securing support for tough colonial policies, the bureaucracy was the visible link between the colonies and Britain and an additional source of uneasiness within the Empire.

The oldest English agency concerned with colonial government was the Privy Council. As late as the reigns of Queen Elizabeth and her successor, James I, the Privy Council was a small and effective body of less than twenty members who advised the monarch and implemented royal policy. Under Charles I (1625–1649) and his son Charles II (1660–1685) the Council lost authority to cliques of favored advisers; the general decline of the king's power following the Revolution of 1688 further reduced the Council's weight; finally, as its size expanded from 52 members in 1714 to 75 in 1760 and 106 in 1782, the Privy Council became an unwieldy ceremonial body that ratified decisions made elsewhere in the executive. Throughout its transformation the Privy Council retained one group of its powers: settling disputes in the colonies between Crown officials and elected assemblies, reviewing all legislation passed by colonial assemblies, and acting as a final appellate court in judicial cases appealed from colonial courts to London for final adjudication. Usually acting on recommendations from the Board of Trade, the Privy Council disallowed many of the laws passed by colonial assemblies and approved by royal governors. The Board of Trade tightened the stringency of disallowance when, beginning in 1720, it instructed royal governors to require that important colonial laws contain a "suspending clause" delaying effectiveness of the statutes until after the Privy Council had reviewed them. The Privy Council's committee on judicial appeals heard, between 1696 and 1783, almost 1,500 appeals on decisions from colonial courts covering a wide variety of cases: white-Indian relations, church-state conflicts, appeals from vice-admiralty courts, and various issues in criminal and civil law. Through disallowance and appellate decisions the Privy Council, working closely with the Board of Trade, had a pervasive impact on colonial law. But the Privy Council encountered increasing difficulty in getting its rulings enforced after 1760, and the complicated, time-consuming nature of the procedure discouraged colonial claimants from appealing cases to London during the last decade of British rule in America.

By far the most important agency formulating colonial policy in the first half of the eighteenth century was the Board of Trade. Created in 1696, the Lords Commissioners of Trade and Plantations, as it was officially titled, devoted much more of its attention to trade than to "plantations" (colonies) and performed the valuable if unexciting task of collecting and evaluating trade statistics and a wide range of information bearing on the economy and politics of the colonies, as well as carrying out some domestic administrative duties. The board drafted instructions to royal governors, and while it had the power to advise the Crown on all royal appointments in the colonies, it effectively controlled only the seats on the royal councils. Periodically the board took up the task of converting faltering proprietary colonies into royal possessions. Between periods of lethargy and drift the board bestirred itself and tried to consolidate its power to become *the* agency controlling all colonial policy and administration. But the House of Commons, still suspicious of the power of the Crown, refused to grant the board's instructions to royal governors the force of law or to punish refractory colonies with coercive legislation.

The Board of Trade did enjoy a resurgence of authority from 1748 to 1761 under the leadership of its president, the Earl of Halifax, who supervised closely the work of governors and other Crown officials. In the first seven years of his tenure on the board, Halifax laid the basis for a sweeping reorganization of colonial government. His plans had to be put aside during the Seven Years' War, when Britain needed colonial cooperation more than it did grudging obedience. (During the Seven Years' War the board did appoint two Superintendents of Indian Affairs, who sought to harmonize the

16 Heroes of the British Empire at the close of the Seven Years' War: George III, Willia[
Pitt, and General James Wolfe, who was mortally wounded in the Battle of Quebec (175[

interests of Indians and the Crown and protect Indian treaty land[
from white encroachment.) Thereafter, no administrator of Ha[
ifax's ability ever undertook direction of colonial policy. Despi[
its failure to centralize the colonial administration and its eclip[
after the Seven Years' War, the board had a profound effect o[
colonial-imperial relations. Over a period of more than sixty yea[
the cluster of financial, legal, and commercial experts who worke[
on the board gradually articulated and elaborated a conception [
the Empire in which the colonies were considered children of th[
parent state, proper subjects of subordination to British power an[
interests. When George III's ministers finally began to tighte[
imperial control after 1760, they found in the old recommen[

28

dations of the Board of Trade a convincing rationale and detailed blueprint for imperial centralization.

The Board of Trade's chief competitor for control of colonial policy was the British Treasury. The king's first minister was customarily First Lord of the Treasury—a forerunner of the modern office of prime minister. As government finance became more complicated and colonial trade burgeoned, Treasury officials moved beyond collecting taxes and auditing records and began to compute the drain that expenditures in the colonies placed on the Treasury. By the 1750s the Crown's operations in America were an accountant's nightmare. Customs receipts under the terms of the acts of trade did not even defray the cost of enforcement. Quitrents, the annual fees paid on land granted by the Crown, were difficult to collect. Most Crown salaries and routine expenditures in the colonies were appropriated by the assemblies, over whose work the Treasury had no control whatever. Armed with voluminous figures about this fiscal chaos, Treasury officials acquired a commanding influence over British colonial policy during the 1760s.

The Treasury also supervised the work of the Board of Customs Commissioners, which collected import and export duties under the Navigation Acts and inspected cargoes leaving colonial ports to determine that enumerated products went only to Britain. Understaffed and underfinanced, the board watched helplessly as an increasing volume of illegal French goods, especially molasses, filled colonial ports. The growing influence of the Treasury and the critical state of British finances after the Seven Years' War emboldened the commissioners to propose in 1763 a wholesale reform of mercantile enforcement procedures: reduction of the molasses duty to a reasonable level and then rigorous enforcement of the new tax; expanded authority to search ships and verify the ultimate destination of enumerated goods; and use of the British navy to eliminate smuggling. The Sugar Act of 1764 put these recommendations into effect and signaled Parliament's intention to impose new imperial control over the colonies.

The Admiralty Board, which was in charge of building and running the navy, was another official body with important colonial

29

responsibilities. The Sugar Act gave the navy the impossible task of enforcing the acts of trade and suppressing smuggling. The great bulk of colonial trade was conducted legally, and such illicit French molasses and lesser amounts of Portuguese wine as reached American waters could easily be transferred to a fishing boat off the coast and unloaded in a quiet cove or inlet at night. Aggressive patrolling and random searching by British naval vessels only angered individualistic captains and merchants. Undermanned and plagued by desertion, the British navy resorted everywhere to impressment, which often incited violent resistance. The Admiralty had also operated, since 1696, eleven vice-admiralty courts in the colonies. Apart from their controversial enforcement of the acts of trade, these courts were efficient and respected by the mercantile community. In wartime they awarded prizes to colonial privateers who seized enemy ships. They adjudicated civil disputes between sailors and captains, tried men accused of crimes on the high seas, and heard cases of alleged smuggling or illegal export of enumerated goods. Acting on complaints by customs officials, the at-

17 Two women pirates convicted in a Jamaica vice-admiralty court in 1720.

torney general for each colony or the court's own advocate general conducted the prosecutions. The courts had no juries, and under the Sugar Act of 1764 vice-admiralty procedure became much more stringent in its prosecution of suspected smugglers. The act placed on the owner of a vessel seized by customs officials the burden of presenting evidence proving that he had not violated the acts of trade. The Sugar Act also directed vice-admiralty judges to rule whether or not customs officials had "just cause" for seizing a ship. If there was due cause, an acquitted defendant could still be forced to pay part of the cost of the prosecution, and he could not sue the customs official for false arrest. Convicted smugglers had their entire cargo confiscated and sold at auction, with customs officials, the vice-admiralty judge, the prosecutor, the governor of the colony, and the king all receiving a share of the proceeds. Vice-admiralty judges received no regular salary, and their income from fees was not considered exorbitant. However, a new breed of officious and overzealous customs officials, sent to the colonies by the Treasury in 1767, discredited both the customs service and the vice-admiralty courts. The American Board of Customs Commissioners, with headquarters in Boston, decided to make an example of the wealthy merchant John Hancock, who had openly boasted that he would "get rid" of them.[3] They seized his ship, the *Liberty* on flimsy evidence. In retaliation, a mob drove the commissioners out of Boston, and the case against Hancock floundered in the Massachusetts vice-admiralty court. A similar episode occurred in Charles Town, South Carolina, where—as we shall see in Chapter 2—an aggressive and unscrupulous customs official attempted a campaign of harassment against Henry Laurens.

Like the Admiralty, the War Office became more deeply involved in colonial administration following the Seven Years' War. For a variety of reasons, the British army left several thousand troops in North America after the Peace of Paris. In part meant to deter Indian aggression and maintain peaceful relations between Indians and whites and also to occupy the newly and unexpectedly acquired territories of French Canada and Spanish Florida, these forces were scattered through Canada and northern New York;

around New York City and neighboring New Jersey, the Ohio Valley, and the Great Lakes; and through the Floridas, Georgia, and South Carolina. The colonists did not at first object to this standing army in peacetime, and the British never seriously considered the implications of leaving troops in the colonies. The colonists' feelings changed, however, when in 1765 Parliament enacted legislation requiring colonies in which troops were stationed to provide barracks or quarters in private homes. Of the more than 5,000 troops in America during the mid-1760s, fewer than 200 were stationed in the more settled parts of Massachusetts, New York, New Jersey, South Carolina, and Georgia; but in all these colonies the assemblies vehemently protested the quartering requirements. These forces were under the command of General Thomas Gage, Commander in Chief of British forces in North America. The division of authority between Gage and the governor in each royal colony seriously weakened the position of both the army and Crown officials. Gage's men could not quell civil disorders unless invited to do so by the governor and his council; governors and councils were afraid to ask unless they knew the army had enough power and numbers to impose order with little bloodshed. During the crisis resulting from the passage of the Stamp Act in 1765, the army—except in Georgia—was impotent. When mob attacks against customs officials in Boston provoked the dispatch of British troops to the city in 1768, their military effectiveness was entirely canceled by the turbulent conditions they encountered. Insulted and abused, the army in Boston became trapped in a rising spiral of animosity and anger that culminated on March 5, 1770, when seven British soldiers fired in apparent self-defense on a hostile crowd. Five people died in what became known as the Boston Massacre.

Finally, the Church of England had a peripheral role in imperial colonial policy. The legally established and predominant church in the South and a rapidly growing and partisan denomination in the middle and New England colonies, the Anglican Church in America came under the jurisdiction of the Bishop of London. Recurring proposals for the creation of an American episcopate, a bishop for the colonies, had for decades ignited arguments about

A MONUMENTAL INSCRIPTION

ON THE

Fifth of March.

Together with a few LINES

On the Enlargement of

EBENEZER RICHARDSON,

Convicted of MURDER.

AMERICANS!
BEAR IN REMEMBRANCE
The HORRID MASSACRE!
Perpetrated in King-ftreet, Boston,
New-England,
On the Evening of March the Fifth, 1770.
When FIVE of your fellow countrymen,
GRAY, MAVERICK, CALDWELL, ATTUCKS,
and CARR,
Lay wallowing in their Gore!
Being *bafely*, and moſt *inhumanly*
MURDERED!
And SIX others badly WOUNDED!
By a Party of the XXIXth Regiment,
Under the command of Capt. Tho. Preſton,
REMEMBER!
That Two of the MURDERERS
Were convicted of MANSLAUGHTER!
By a Jury, of whom I ſhall ſay
NOTHING,
Branded in the hand!
And *difmiffed*,
The others were ACQUITTED,
And their Captain PENSIONED!
Alſo,
BEAR IN REMEMBRANCE
That on the 22d Day of February, 1770,
The infamous
EBENEZER RICHARDSON, Informer,
And tool to Miniſterial hirelings,
Moſt *barbarouſly*
MURDERED
CHRISTOPHER SEIDER,
An innocent youth!
Of which crime he was found guilty
By his Country
On Friday April 20th, 1770;
But remained *Unfentenced*
On Saturday the 22d Day of February, 1772.
When the GRAND INQUEST
For Suffolk county,
Were informed, at requeſt,
By the Judges of the Superior Court,
That EBENEZER RICHARDSON'S *Cafe*
Then lay before his MAJESTY.
Therefore ſaid *Richardfon*
This day, MARCH FIFTH! 1772,
Remains UNHANGED!!!
Let THESE things be told to Poſterity!
And handed down
From Generation to Generation,
'Till Time ſhall be no more!
Forever may AMERICA be preſerved,
From weak and wicked monarchs,
Tyrannical Miniſters,
Abandoned Governors,
Their Underlings and Hirelings!
And may the
Machinations of artful, *defigning* wretches,
Who would ENSLAVE THIS People,
Come to an end,
Let their NAMES and MEMORIES
Be buried in eternal oblivion,
And the PRESS,
For a *SCOURGE* to Tyrannical Rulers,
Remain FREE.

AWAKE my drowſy Thoughts! Awake my muſe!
Awake O earth, and tremble at the news!
In grand defiance to the laws of God,
The Guilty, Guilty murd'rer walks abroad.
That city mourns, (the cry comes from the ground,)
Where law and juſtice never can be found:
Oh! ſword of vengeance, fall thou on the race
Of thoſe who hinder juſtice from its place.
O MURD'RER! RICHARDSON! with their lateſt breath
Millions will curſe you when you ſleep in death!
Infernal horrors ſure will ſhake your ſoul
When o'er your head the awful thunders roll.
Earth cannot hide you, always will the cry
Of Murder! Murder! haunt you 'till you die!
To yonder grave! with trembling joints repair,
Remember, SEIDER's corps lies mould'ring there;
There drop a tear, and think what you have done!
Then judge how you can live beneath the Sun.
A PARDON may arrive! You laws defy,
But Heaven's laws will ſtand when KINGS ſhall die.
Oh! Wretched man! the monſter of the times,
You were not hung " by reaſon of *old* Lines,"
Old Lines thrown by, 'twas then we were in hopes,
That you would ſoon be hung with *new made* Ropes ✳
But neither *Ropes nor Lines*, will ſatisfy
For SEIDER's blood! But GOD is ever nigh,
And guilty ſouls will not unpuniſh'd go
Tho' they're excus'd by judges here below!
You are enlarg'd but curſed is your fate
Tho' *Cufhing*'s eas'd you from the priſon gate
The ⁂*Bridge* of *Tories*, it has borne you o'er
Yet you e'er long may meet with HELL's dark ſhore.

✳ *Lins*. the name of one of the judges
✱ Name of another judge newly named
† Do. of another of the judges
⁂ *Trowbridge* another judge

18   A 1772 broadside commemorating the anniversary of the Boston Massacre.

the sinister political motives of the Anglican Church and had kept alive the specter of a privileged church using its influence among Crown officials to undermine Congregationalist, Presbyterian, and other dissenting denominations. Although nothing ever came of ... talk of an American bishop, the church's Society for the Propagation of the Gospel in Foreign Parts (known simply as the S.P.G.) appeared to have real political influence. It sent scores of missionaries to the colonies, first to Christianize the Indians, and when that project fizzled, to establish episcopal congregations in the heartland of dissenter strength, New England and the middle colonies.

PARLIAMENT, THE CABINET, AND IMPERIAL CONTROL

While these agencies each had a share of the task of governing the Empire and day to day, in many small ways, shaped colonial policy, the ultimate determination of that policy rested in two intertwined institutions: Parliament, particularly the House of Commons, and the ministry, more specifically the small group of ministers known as the Cabinet. From the accession of the Hanoverians to the British throne in 1714 until the 1760s, ministries and Parliaments had enjoyed an era of harmony and enlarged responsibility. There were occasional fierce struggles for power and some controversial legislation, but the great controversies of the seventeenth century over church-state relations and the supremacy of Parliament had all been put to rest by 1714; only after 1815 did lower- and middle-class political leaders rise to demand a share of political power. The nation's government rested in the hands of an established and widely accepted oligarchy of landowners and professional men who had either won election to the House of Commons by a restricted and unevenly distributed electorate, inherited seats in the House of Lords, been raised to the peerage by the king, or secured executive or judicial appointments on the basis of ability and connections. The questions that agitated these men concerned patronage, foreign policy, and the periodic waging of war. During the reigns of George I and George II neither Parliaments nor ministries got around very often to dealing with broad issues of colonial policy. In the 1760s, however, colonial policy became one of the most vexing issues in British politics and placed a heavy drain on the time and energy of ministers.

The membership of the House of Commons was a mixture of aristocrats, merchants, lawyers, military officers, political operators, and Crown officeholders. They were not organized into government and opposition parties (although opposition members did sit together across from the Treasury bench); instead, the eighteenth-century House of Commons consisted of temporary and

19 Cartoon depicting a debate in the House of Commons.

shifting alignments. "Placemen," or holders of Crown jobs, were the most stable element; they constituted a relatively reliable source of votes for the ministry of the day because they owed allegiance to the king and to his ministers. If the king and his leading ministers had a falling-out, the placemen would attempt to side with the probable winner of the contest. Ministers and other factional leaders had their own personal followings—voluntary members of their faction, relatives, friends, dependents. But the independent country gentlemen, who felt assured of reelection to the House and owed their loyalty to no man, made up a large floating vote that could not be controlled by the Crown or the leaders of factions. To govern, the king had to construct a ministry that he could trust, that had the support of a broad coalition of factional leaders and that would not blunder so badly as to antagonize the high-minded country gentlemen. To keep a majority of the Commons in line, ministries spent a great deal of time proposing and shepherding through Parliament mundane legislation designed to satisfy particular interests: turnpike construction, licensing of public houses, trade regulations, and details of inheritance, property, and commercial law.

The initiation of legislation in Parliament rested with those members of both houses who belonged to the Cabinet. This body had originated in the late seventeenth century when an intimate committee of the Privy Council was formed to deal with matters requiring the attention of a small and discreet group. Gradually, during the first half of the eighteenth century, the "cabinet council," as it was called, became more and more powerful; but, like the Privy Council before it, this body also became too large and cumbersome. In 1757, during the Seven Years' War, an "inner" cabinet of the most important ministers convened to deal with major questions of policy. Between 1760 and 1765 this body shrank from more than twelve to between seven and nine members and tried to exercise effective control over the formulation and implementation of military, diplomatic, and colonial policies.

During the 1760s, as we have seen, there were a succession of ministers—such as Grenville and Townshend—who favored tightening control over the colonies. Under their leadership the main responsibility for determining colonial policy shifted from the old departments, boards, and committees of imperial bureaucracy into the hands of the Cabinet itself, especially the Chancellor of the Exchequer, the Secretary of State for the Southern Department, and, starting in 1768, the new post of Colonial Secretary. At long last, colonial affairs came under high-level scrutiny by the Cabinet and the colonial secretary's staff, called the American Department. The shift was achieved by the clique of professional colonial experts who had worked as subministers at the Treasury and the Board of Trade and who after 1768 would serve in the American Department—chiefly Thomas Whately, William Knox, John Pownall, and John Robinson. These men had spent years mastering the intricacies of imperial administration and formulating new and tough colonial policies. When their patron and ally, George Grenville, became the king's first minister and chancellor of the exchequer in 1763, they provided him with the detailed arguments and proposals he needed to tighten control over the colonies. The result of these developments was a new colonial policy—on which several high-ranking ministers staked their careers—prepared by a shadowy group of subministerial advisers who firmly believed that the colonies had reached a dangerous degree of autonomy and that survival of the Empire required a strong dose of centralization and control.

The effect of these centrifugal forces in British politics was to enhance the power of a new breed of men who had real experience in the workings of bureaucracy, the patience to initiate and execute a complex program of imperial centralization, and a belief that they were applying reason to the chaotic state of colonial life. As professionals they lacked the brilliance, quick sympathies, and intuitive sensitivity that often characterize the political amateur. When George Grenville became the king's first minister, he went to work to implement the long-standing proposals of professional bureaucrats in the Treasury and Board of Trade for imperial centralization. The four main acts that constituted his program were the Sugar Act of 1764, which tightened at every level the enforcement of the acts of trade; the Currency Act of 1764, which forbade further emissions of legal tender paper money by colonial assemblies; the Quartering Act of 1765, which required the colonial assemblies to provide barracks or other housing for British troops in the colonies; and, most serious of all, the Stamp Act of 1765, which required the use of taxed stamps on newspapers and legal documents.

These enactments first bewildered, then stunned, and soon provoked radical protest by a broad spectrum of colonial opinion. The Currency Act seemed to emasculate the assemblies' ability to provide legislative relief for an urgent public need for an expanded money supply. The inability of merchants and royal officials with good connections in Britain to secure reconsideration of the Sugar Act was an ominous indication than Anglo-American political connections could no longer significantly benefit the colonists. The Stamp Act in particular provoked a volcanic eruption of protest. "No taxation without representation" was more than a slogan; it was a matter of societal life and death. Government depended for its very legitimacy and survival on its ability to protect its subjects from arbitrary seizures of their property. Once the exclusive power to tax was wrested from the colonial assemblies and transferred to a remote, arrogant, or perhaps indifferent Parliament, colonial politics would become an irrational nightmare instead of a collective search for the common good. The opponents of the Stamp Act brought royal authority to virtual collapse; they closed courts, burned stamp distributors in effigy, sacked the homes of the stamp distributor and the lieutenant governor of Massachusetts, intimidated distributors into resignation, prevented distribution of the stamps, defied the British army in New York City, halted trade with Great Britain, and elected an extra-legal Stamp Act Congress to speak for the whole colonial populace. It was coincidental that Grenville fell from power over a trifling dispute with George III on the eve of colonial response to the Stamp Act. The king had no choice but to ask Lord Rockingham, who had a large circle of correspondents in the colonies and was keenly aware of the damage the Grenville program had done to the colonists' affection for Britain, to form a government. Aristocratic, haughty, and airily contemptuous of Grenville's colonial policy, the cluster of Parliamentary figures known as the Rockingham Whigs had no intention of making bargains with the king's friends or with any other Parliamentary faction in order to remain in power, and they envisioned a general loosening of colonial policy. Weakened by their own hauteur, the king's disdain, and Pitt's refusal to support them, they stayed in office only long enough to maneuver tortuously through Parliament the repeal of the Stamp Act, and only then at the cost of an accompanying Declaratory Act affirming Parliament's power to legislate for the colonies on any subject.

If ever there was a ministry with the talent needed to reconcile the colonies to Britain, it was that of William Pitt, now the Earl of Chatham, who became the king's first minister in 1766 after Rockingham fell from power. Pitt had finally won the trust and affection of the king by agreeing to help rid British politics of the evil influence of *party*—factions that owed their loyalty to a single leader. Consequently, Pitt, who had vociferously denounced the Stamp Act, collaborated with the king in forming a ministry that within six months almost totally excluded the Rockingham Whigs from power. The new Secretary of State for the Southern Department was Pitt's confidant, the Earl of Shelburne. An aloof, shy intellectual, Shelburne had a vague but highly intelligent plan to harmonize the economic interests of Britain with those of the colonies. He intended to foster expansion west of the Appalachians and to reorganize the distribution of land grants and the collection of quitrents. The resulting proceeds of expanded and carefully administered land distribution would pay the soaring new costs of imperial defense, including the larger western garrisons needed under Shelburne's plan to keep the Indians at peace. Land-grant fees and quitrents would raise none of the thorny constitutional issues created by Parliamentary taxation of the colonies. Pitt's long record of sympathy for colonial attitudes and Shelburne's bold new colonial policy ought, by any calculation, to have reversed the deterioration of relations with the colonies.

But Shelburne did not function well in the shifting, uncertain political conditions of the mid-1760s; and Pitt's painful illness and virtual mental collapse made him a powerless figurehead. Moving impulsively to fill this vacuum in 1767, Chancellor of the Exchequer Charles Townshend pushed through Parliament a series of coercive measures over Shelburne's opposition: suspension of the New York assembly for refusing to quarter British troops, creation of a new and more powerful American Board of Customs Commissioners, and the Townshend duties, which were new revenue-producing taxes on colonial imports from Britain of tea, glass, lead, silk, paper, and paint. The final blow for Shelburne was the division of his Cabinet post into two positions, Colonial Secretary and Secretary of State for the Southern Department. Given his choice of the two, he retained the latter title; he had given up hope of reforming colonial policy, and consequently the job went to The Earl of Hillsborough, an obtuse but industrious minister who spent his four years in the post scolding royal governors who showed any sign of flexibility in dealing with their assemblies.

The colonial reaction to Townshend's program was less effective and more ambiguous than the Stamp Act protests. On February 11, 1768, the Massachusetts House of Representatives sent a circular letter to the other assemblies attacking the new measures. Hillsborough was so offended that he ordered royal governors to prorogue or dissolve any assembly that tried to discuss the letter. That tactless and unenforceable order in turn so offended the assemblies that they enthusiastically considered and endorsed the Massachusetts appeal. Capitalizing on this show of unity, popular leaders in Boston, New York, and Philadelphia throughout the summer of 1768 outmaneuvered the cautious members of the merchant community and aroused enough support to impose a nonimportation boycott on British goods taxed by the Townshend duties. Trying to redeem the situation, Britain in early 1770 repealed all of the Townshend duties except the one on tea, and by October 1770 nonimportation collapsed amid bitter recriminations between Boston and New York City.

Lord North, who had been chosen to head the government in 1770 and whose ministry would last for the next twelve years, consolidated his government in 1772 by giving the colonial secretaryship to Lord Dartmouth after Hillsborough had stepped down.

20　A drawing of seventeen Massachusetts Tories marching into hell after they had voted to rescind the Massachusetts Circular Letter.

A Rockingham Whig, Dartmouth was too gentle and politically weakened to fight for a change in colonial policy. When North pushed the Tea Act through Parliament—giving the financially shaky East India Company a monopoly of the tea trade in the colonies and leading eventually to the Boston Tea Party (to be discussed in Chapter 2)—he did not even consult Dartmouth. And when the Coercive Acts punished Massachusetts for the destruction of the tea, Dartmouth sadly went along with the new legislation in the vague hope that it would have a sobering effect on the colonists and help produce a reconciliation.

THE IDEOLOGY OF EMPIRE

The men who governed the Empire—the king and his ministers, members of Parliament, and officeholders in the imperial bureaucracy—were not unthinking automatons. They brought to their work an intelligent body of ideas and purposes. They believed in the supremacy of Parliament and, more broadly, in the need for the

41

Crown to exercise sufficient power in the colonies to contain the natural restiveness of the people there. They believed that the colonies were a vital economic and military asset to Great Britain and, therefore, that the regulation of imperial trade, the financing of imperial government, and the preservation of colonial subordination in areas of trade and finance were ultimately the responsibility of the British government. What they lacked was a theory explaining why conflicts developed between Britain and the colonies and what limitations impinged on Britain's power to resolve those conflicts.

The sovereignty of Parliament was one of the modern triumphs of political ingenuity and intellect. A century of constitutional struggle in England between the Parliament and Stuart monarchs culminated in the Revolution of 1688, the establishment of a Protestant succession to the British throne, and the establishment of Parliamentary supremacy. In his classic treatise *Commentaries on the Laws of England,* published during the 1760s, English jurist Sir William Blackstone argued authoritatively that "no power on earth can undo" what the Commons, Lords, and King agreed should be the law of the realm. On this issue there was no partisan disagreement; even the most stalwart defenders of colonial liberty, in the House of Commons, admitted Parliament's power to legislate for the colonies. As long as Parliament left colonial policy in the hands of the Privy Council and the Board of Trade and refused to endow the royal instructions with the force of law, Parliamentary power did not disturb Americans. But once Parliament enacted into law the Treasury's program for governing the colonies—the Sugar and Currency acts of 1764 and the Stamp Act of 1765—the lines of authority and control over the colonies abruptly tightened, and further extensions of Parliamentary power through the Townshend duties and the Tea Act became almost inevitable.

The resulting controversy over Parliamentary power and colonial rights brought to the surface a long-hidden but serious disagreement about the role of the Crown itself in the colonial constitutional order. During the early seventeenth century in England there had been two rival interpretations of the power of the Crown: the early Stuarts' view that the king's *will* and volition alone guaranteed liberty and representative government, and Parliament's insistence that the power of the Crown was a *custom* in English political life that had evolved according to the needs of the kingdom in each generation. Once Parliament gained the upper hand in its struggle with the Crown following the Revolution of 1688, it no longer needed to justify its pretensions and ceased using the doctrine of custom to justify its conduct. In the colonies, however, the clash of custom and will continued. Many imperial officials continued to assume that their authority came directly from the king and that the function of royal policy was to check and oppose tendencies toward colonial autonomy. During the eighteenth century the colonists increasingly responded that local customs, practice, and precedent limited and opposed those very pretensions to supreme power. Both sides agreed that the Crown was the legitimate executive branch of colonial government and that the colonists should participate in the operation of colonial government. They disagreed about the ultimate source of executive authority, some royal officials tracing it to the will of the monarch and most colonial leaders to a compact between the Crown and the colony.

A few thoughtful men within the imperial system sensed the need for a concept of Empire that acknowledged forthrightly the potential for conflict between the British and the colonists. Francis Bernard, Governor of Massachusetts, composed in 1763 a series of ninety-seven propositions warning of disastrous dissidence if Britain imposed new policies on the colonies as they were then constituted. First, he pleaded, Britain needed to win the confidence and support of influential men in every colony. The creation of a colonial nobility, a voluntary agreement between the colonies and Britain about a colonial contribution toward the cost of imperial defense, and a reorganization of colonial governments to make them more efficient, popular, and uniform were the preliminary steps necessary before Britain imposed new taxes and restrictions on the colonies. Bernard acknowledged the supremacy of Parliament and wanted to invigorate the authority of the Crown. He certainly expected the adoption of these recommendations to advance his own career. But he sensed as well that many colonists were ready to help improve, reform, and rationalize the machinery of government in America if only Britain would approach them in an open, respectful manner. In this way alone could the authority of Parliament and the Crown be set on a firm foundation. To Bernard's disappointment his recommendations were ignored by officials in London.

Bernard's predecessor as governor of Massachusetts, Thomas Pownall, published in 1764 a long treatise, *The Administration of the Colonies,* which he reissued and revised five times in the following decade. Pownall's study argued that the Empire should become a more rational enterprise, in which mutual commercial prosperity rather than legality cemented the colonies to Britain. He pleaded for British officials to approach controversies with the colonies in a conciliatory and generous frame of mind. He skirted the vital issues of Parliament's power to tax the colonies and the extent of the Crown's authority there. Like Bernard, Pownall recognized that the early 1760s had been the last chance to strengthen and nourish the ties of the Empire. He seemed to realize, with regret, that his ideas were a little too late to alter the course of events. The presence of men like Pownall and Bernard in the imperial establishment, however, as well as the serious efforts of men throughout the system to justify the use of Parliamentary and prerogative power in the colonies, suggests that British imperial thinking was not a stagnant, conventional orthodoxy, but that it was rigid, limited, and applied by men of restricted vision and ability.

The Empire never recovered from the trials and triumphs of the Seven Years' War—a conflict increasingly known to historians as "the great war for Empire." The whole experience of managing the Empire during the war—maintaining an army in a frontier wilderness, cultivating Indian alliances and regulating white-Indian relations, and finally facing up to the hard financial realities created by the conquest of a vast territory—concentrated the thinking of British officials and statesmen, limited their options, and hardened their attitudes. The war thrust British leaders down the path of imperial centralization backed by the power of Parliament and the Crown. The struggle had just the reverse meaning for the colonists. They were proud of their contribution to British victory. Pitt's concessions to the colonial assemblies gave the legislatures a new measure of self-confidence and authority. Colonial troops resented the condescending attitude of British regulars. Wartime prosperity and postwar depression only made the economic impact of the Grenville program more galling.

Notes

[1] The terms "English" and "British" appear frequently in this chapter. From 1603 to 1707 England and Scotland were separate countries but shared the same monarch. In 1707 the two were joined into the single kingdom of Great Britain.
[2] Quoted in Jack P. Greene, *The Quest for Power* (Chapel Hill: University of North Carolina Press, 1963), p. 15.
[3] Quoted in Thomas C. Barrow, *Trade and Empire* (Cambridge: Harvard University Press, 1967), p. 230.

Bibliography

The best introductions to the study of the British Empire are Jack P. Greene, ed., *Great Britain and the American Colonies, 1606–1763* (New York: Harper and Row, 1970), pp. xi–xlvii; Lawrence H. Gipson, "The American Revolution as an Aftermath of the Great War for Empire," *Political Science Quarterly,* LXV (1950), 86–104; and Peter Marshall, "The British Empire and the American Revolution, *Huntington Library Quarterly,* XXVII (1964), 135–45. The major scholarly studies of the Empire are Lawrence H. Gipson, *The British Empire Before the American Revolution,* 15 vols. (New York: Alfred Knopf, 1936–1970), and Charles M. Andrews, *The Colonial Period of American History,* 4 vols. (New Haven: Yale University Press, 1934–1938). Recent assessments of the internal stresses in the machinery of the Empire include Michael Kammen, *Empire and Interest: The American Colonies and the Politics of Mercantilism* (Philadelphia: J. B. Lippincott, 1970); Jack P. Greene, "An Uneasy Connection: An Analysis of the Preconditions of the American Revolution," in Stephen G. Kurtz and James H. Hutson, eds., *Essays on the American Revolution* (Chapel Hill: University of North Carolina Press, 1973); and two documentary articles edited by Jack P. Greene: "William Knox's Explanation for the American Revolution" and "Social Structure and Political Behavior

45

in Revolutionary America: John Day's *Remarks on American Affairs,"* *William and Mary Quarterly* (hereafter cited as *WMQ*), XXX (1973), 293–306, and XXXII (1975), 471–94.

On specific agencies of imperial administration, see John Shy, *Toward Lexington: The Role of the British Army in the Coming of the Revolution* (Princeton: Princeton University Press, 1965); Dora Mae Clark, *The Rise of the British Treasury: Colonial Administration in the Eighteenth Century* (New Haven: Yale University Press, 1960); Joseph Henry Smith, *Appeals to the Privy Council from the American Plantations* (New York: Columbia University Press, 1950); Thomas C. Barrow, *Trade and Empire: The British Customs Service in Colonial America, 1660–1775* (Cambridge: Harvard University Press, 1967); Carl Ubbelohde, *The Vice Admiralty Courts and the American Revolution* (Chapel Hill: University of North Carolina Press, 1960). On the American Department, see Franklin B. Wickwire, *British Subministers and Colonial America, 1763–1783* (Princeton: Princeton University Press, 1966), and Charles R. Ritcheson, *British Politics and the American Revolution* (Norman: University of Oklahoma Press, 1954). On the role of the Board of Trade, see Charles M. Andrews, *The Colonial Period of American History,* vol. 4 (New Haven: Yale University Press, 1938) 272–315, 377–423, and Thomas C. Barrow, "Background to the Grenville Program, 1757–1763," *WMQ*, XXII (1965), 92–104.

On British politics and the coming of the Revolution, Jack P. Greene, "The Plunge of Lemmings: A Consideration of Recent Writings on British Politics and the American Revolution," *South Atlantic Quarterly,* LVII (1968), 141–75 examines the influence of Sir Lewis Namier on the historiography of the Revolution and discusses a large number of recent books on the subject; of these the most useful are Bernard Donaughue, *British Politics and the American Revolution: The Path to War, 1773–1775* (London: Macmillan, 1964); John Brook, *The Chatham Administration, 1766–1768* (London: Macmillan, 1956); John Brook and Lewis Namier, *Charles Townshend* (London: Macmillan, 1964); Bradley Bargar, *Lord Dartmouth and the American Revolution* (Columbia: University of South Carolina Press, 1965); John Norris, *Shelburne and Reform* (London: Macmillan, 1963); and Jack M. Sosin, *Whitehall and the Wilderness: The Middle West in British Policy, 1760–1775* (Lincoln: University of Nebraska Press, 1961).

Special studies of the British West Indies have thrown a great deal of new light on the influence of wealth and slavery on imperial development; see especially Richard S. Dunn, *Sugar and Slavery: The Rise of the Planter Class in the English West Indies, 1624–1713* (Chapel Hill: University of North Carolina Press, 1972); Carl and Roberta Bridenbaugh, *No Peace Beyond the Line: The English in the Caribbean, 1624–1690* (New York: Oxford University Press, 1972); and Richard B. Sheridan, *Sugar and Slav-*

ery: An Economic History of the British West Indies, 1623–1775 (Baltimore: Johns Hopkins University Press, 1974).

A variety of specialized studies probe the politics of colonial-imperial relations. Leonard W. Babaree, *Royal Government in America* (New Haven: Yale University Press, 1930) remains the foundation on which subsequent scholarship rests. Alison G. Olson and Richard M. Brown, eds., *Anglo-American Political Relations, 1675–1775* (New Brunswick, N. J.: Rutgers University Press, 1970) examines the network of informal trans-Atlantic relationships linking British officials and colonial politicians until the 1750s and the breakdown of that network during the pre-Revolutionary period. Alison G. Olson, *Anglo-American Politics, 1660–1775: The Relationship Between Parties in England and Colonial America* (New York: Oxford University Press, 1973) suggests that imperial tensions helped create factional political conflict in both England and the colonies. Michael Kammen, *A Rope of Sand: Colonial Agents, British Politics, and the American Revolution* (Ithaca: Cornell University Press, 1968) depicts colonial agents as victims of ministerial power politics; in contrast, Jack M. Sosin, *Agents and Merchants: British Colonial Policy and the Origins of the American Revolution, 1763–1775* (Lincoln: University of Nebraska Press, 1965) blames ministerial difficulties, in part, on the shortsightedness and opportunism of the agents. Oliver M. Dickerson, *The Navigation Acts and the American Revolution* (Philadelphia: University of Pennsylvania Press, 1951) argues that the acts of trade were the "cement of Empire" until 1763, and that during the late 1760s arbitrary enforcement destroyed colonial acceptance of the acts. In a very different analysis of economic interests and political behavior, Joseph Albert Ernst, *Money and Politics: A Study of the Currency Act of 1764 and the Political Economy of the Revolution* (Chapel Hill: University of North Carolina Press, 1973) blames periodic liquidity crises, when colonial merchants could not meet their sterling obligations, for colonial disenchantment with British rule.

Resistance 2

In behalf of European liberalism the revolutionary leaders undertook to complete, sys-
tematize, and symbolize what previously had
been only partially realized, confused and
disputed matters of fact. . . . This comple-
tion, this rationalization, this symbolization,
this lifting into consciousness and endowing
with high moral purpose inchoate, confused
elements of social and political change—this
was the American Revolution.*

Bernard Bailyn

THE COURSE OF EVENTS, 1767–1776

Repeal of the Stamp Act in 1766 did not alleviate the basic constitutional impasse between Britain and the colonies. The accompanying Declaratory Act reiterated Parliamentary supremacy over the
colonies, and the Townshend duties reimposed Parliamentary taxation—this time under the authority of Parliament's well-
established power to regulate trade. News of the Townshend duties
reached the colonies in September 1767, and more than a year of
debate and acrimony transpired before merchants in the major
ports reluctantly agreed to boycott British goods taxed under the

* Bernard Bailyn, "Political Experience and Enlightenment Ideas in Eighteenth-
Century America," *American Historical Review*, LXVII (1962), 351.

THE PATRIOTIC AMERICAN FARMER.
J-N D-K-NS——N Esqr BARRISTER at LAW:
*Who with Attic Eloquence and Roman Spirit hath Asserted,
The Liberties of the* BRITISH *Colonies in America.*

'Tis nobly done, to stem Taxations Rage,
And raise, the thoughts of a degen'rate Age,
For Happiness, and Joy, from Freedom Spring;
But Life in Bondage, is a worthless Thing.

Printed for & Sold by R. Bell. Bookseller

21 John Dickinson, author of *Letters of a Pennsylvania Farmer*, who was characterized by John Adams as "slender as a reed, pale as ashes."

new act. New York imposed nonimportation on November 1, 1768; Boston, which had been the first to advocate nonimportation but could not act unless other cities supported her, instituted the boycott on January 1, 1769; Philadelphia complied in March and Charles Town in July. Elsewhere compliance was spotty, and in the four major ports merchants secretly replenished their stocks of proscribed British goods. Partial repeal of the Townshend duties in early 1770, leaving only the duty on tea, satisfied none of the colonial objections to the act, but disunity and frustration made it impossible to sustain the boycott, which collapsed in the autumn of 1770.

Nevertheless, the Townshend-duties crisis contributed significantly to the colonists' capacity for resistance and confrontation. John Dickinson's *Letters of a Pennsylvania Farmer*, published in late 1767 and early 1768 in Philadelphia and reprinted widely in newspaper columns and pamphlets, provided a sophisticated analysis of British policy in the 1760s. The Townshend duties, he argued, were no isolated British encroachment but part of a concerted, diabolical plan to enslave the colonies. Dickinson's suspicions were justified. The Townshend duties were the last step in a comprehensive program to secure colonial subordination; other measures included the suspension of the New York assembly for refusing to provide barracks for British troops, the creation of a new American Board of Customs Commissioners headquartered in Boston and given increased enforcement powers, and the decision to earmark revenue from the Townshend duties to pay royal salaries to Crown officials and thereby free them from dependence on salaries from their assemblies. The decision to dispatch British

22 An engraving by Paul Revere depicting the 1768 landing of British troops in Boston.

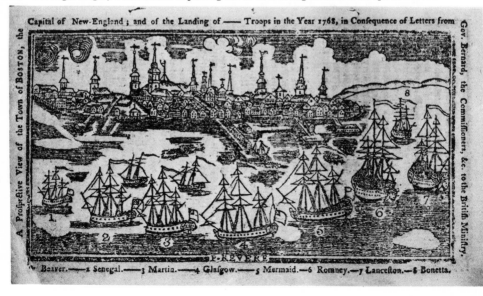

troops to Boston, following the stoning of customs officials there in 1768, was a natural extension of the Townshend program. The repeated clashes between soldiers and civilians in Boston in 1769 and 1770, culminating in the Boston Massacre and trials of the British soldiers for manslaughter, focused attention on British conduct throughout the colonies and helped sustain opposition to the Townshend duties.

In contrast with 1765–1766 and 1768–1770, the period from 1771 to 1773 seemed like a time of quiet in imperial colonial relations. There were, to be sure, disputes involving serious constitutional issues—in South Carolina over whether the assembly could spend money outside of the colony without the consent of the governor and council, and in Massachusetts over the governor's removal of the assembly from its traditional seat in Boston to quarters in Cambridge as a disciplinary measure—but these disputes did not generate the emotion necessary to sustain a mass movement of resistance.

Throughout the spring of 1772 Lieutenant William Duddington and the crew of H.M.S. *Gaspee* patrolled the Rhode Island coast arbitrarily searching ships, shooting at fishermen, stealing livestock, and generally, in historian David S. Lovejoy's words, "making themselves as obnoxious as pirates."[1] While in pursuit of a coastal vessel on the afternoon of June 9, 1772, the *Gaspee* ran aground near the town of Warwick, Rhode Island. A body of townspeople in small boats surrounded the ship, shot and wounded Duddington, took him and his crew off the vessel, and burned it to the waterline. This outrage provoked the Crown to send a commission of inquiry into the colony. It found insufficient evidence to identify the culprits, but even this intervention into Rhode Island affairs was sufficiently alarming to cause the creation of committees of correspondence in ten colonial assemblies to exchange views about British measures and intentions.

In 1773 the brief period of comparative calm in British-colonial relations came to an end, and one of those most involved in events that gave rise to the change was Thomas Hutchinson. He had worked for a lifetime to become governor of Massachusetts, and he

23 Thomas Hutchinson, age 30, by Edward Truman.

endured the torments of the 1760s as the leading apologist for British policy because he yearned to preside over the return of tranquility to the colony. At the very time that his appointment as governor was approved in 1771 by London, Hutchinson decided to retire from public life. Only with the greatest difficulty did Colonial Secretary Hillsborough persuade him to accept the new appointment. Hutchinson realized, perhaps better than anyone else in the Empire, that controversy about the legitimate extent of Parliamentary power and uncertainty on the part of the colonists about the Crown's willingness to impose its authority on them were an acid destroying the habits and traditions of the Empire. Only swift imposition of coercion and then a long period of healing and moderation, he concluded, could repair the damage. Hutchinson doubted whether he had the strength and toughness to carry out such a program, and he feared that British leaders lacked the sophistication and foresight to conceive of the problem in those terms.

The Tea Act of 1773 confirmed Hutchinson's assessment of ministerial imagination. The act was a sensible solution to a vexing and interrelated set of financial and political problems—but one that took no account of colonial sensibilities. The East India Company was on the verge of bankruptcy. No British government could allow a major economic enterprise, established by a charter from the Crown and responsible for a large part of the wealth of the nation, to collapse. The act granted the company a monopoly in the tea export trade to the North American colonies; it retained the Townshend duty on tea but allowed the company to sell directly to its own colonial agents rather than auction in the colonial market to any bidder. The act promised to save the East India Company from ruin and to insure its future profitability. Moreover, it seemed destined to remove colonial resistance to the Townshend duty on tea by providing a single, cheap source of that product at a price that undersold smuggled Dutch tea. As we shall see in the discussion of the techniques of resistance in this chapter, the act provided popular leaders with just the dramatic grievance needed to create new mass protests against British policy.

In retaliation for the destruction of the first shipment of tea sent to Boston under the new act, Parliament passed in the spring of 1774 four Coercive Acts—called the "Intolerable Acts" by the colonists—designed to punish Boston. The Boston Port Act closed the port of Boston to all normal commerce until the town paid for the destroyed tea; an Administration of Justice Act provided that Crown officials accused of committing crimes in Massachusetts would be returned to England for trial; a Quartering Act perpetuated the power of the British army to house troops in unoccupied public buildings. Most serious of all, the Massachusetts Government Act gutted the 1691 charter of the colony by abolishing the elected council and replacing it with a royally appointed body, giving the governor power to dismiss sheriffs, justices of the peace, and lower court judges, and prohibiting towns from holding more than a single town meeting each year without special permission.

At this time an act dealing with the civil government of Quebec also passed, and because it established an autocratic government, aspects of Roman civil law, and Catholicism in Quebec and extended Quebec's borders into land in the Ohio Valley also claimed by Massachusetts, Virginia, and Connecticut, patriots also considered it a part of the Intolerable Acts.

After a certain amount of maneuvering, radicals in Boston and more cautious leaders in New York and Philadelphia agreed to hold a general continental congress. Moderates hoped that the meeting would repeat the performance of the Stamp Act Congress of 1765, which had stated colonial grievances and then adjourned; more militant colonial leaders hoped that the congress would be a step toward demands that Britain repeal the Coercive Acts and abandon its infringements on colonial liberty. When the First Continental Congress met in Philadelphia in September 1774, a broad consensus between these two views quickly developed. The congress denounced practically all British laws and regulations affecting the colonies that had been enacted since 1763; it postponed consideration of a Plan of Union put forward by Joseph Galloway of Pennsylvania that called for an American branch of the British Parliament and much closer integration of colonial and imperial political institutions; it voted to halt all importation from Britain on December 1, 1774, to boycott the consumption of British products on March 1, 1775, and to cease exports to Britain on September 1, 1775. Most extreme of all, the First Congress endorsed resolutions that originated in the Suffolk County, Massachusetts, Convention and called on the people to disobey the Coercive Acts, take tax collection into their own hands, and form a militia, as well as using economic retaliation against Britain.

Powerless to prevent the spontaneous creation of county and town committees of safety to enforce nonimportation, royal governors saw their authority collapse during the winter of 1774–1775. There were, to be sure, deep divisions within colonial society. In January 1775 the New York assembly refused to endorse the work of the First Continental Congress. That spring more than 1,400 North Carolinians signed petitions vindicating British authority.

24 A meeting of the First Continental Congress, as imagined in a French engraving.

Georgia failed to support nonimportation. But royal officials were unable to capitalize on these divisions. Committees became a law unto themselves. They were remarkably thorough in uncovering violators and even critics of the boycott and in exposing these people to public scorn, censure, and physical danger. The inability of royal governors to protect their own supporters from such indignities marked the effective breakdown of royal government.

In Massachusetts, Hutchinson had been replaced by General Gage, who, with British troops patrolling Boston, was in effect a military governor. On·October 7, 1774, the assembly met in Salem in defiance of Gage, who had not authorized the meeting. The legislators then retired to the interior and became a Provincial Congress, which in turn created a committee of safety and took control of the colony's militia. Alarmed by the military preparations of the Provincial Congress and under orders from London to

25 Carpenter's Hall, Philadelphia, meeting place of the First Continental Congress.

Carpenters Hall Phil^a in which the first U S Congress sat in 1775

use force to stem the deterioration of British authority, Gage dispatched British regulars to seize rebel arms in Concord. As we shall see in Chapter 3, fighting ensued and a state of war commenced. Against this background the Second Continental Congress assembled in Philadelphia on May 10, 1775. Congress voted to take up arms as a defensive measure against further British aggression and named George Washington to command the hodgepodge of militia surrounding the city of Boston. Congress also made a last gesture of conciliation, passing the Olive Branch petition, which acknowledged American allegiance and called on George III to halt further attempts to suppress colonial resistance.

In response, the king declared on August 23, 1775, that the colonies were in a state of rebellion. Congress prepared for war, creating a navy and appointing agents to seek European aid in the coming struggle. The publication in Philadelphia of Thomas Paine's *Common Sense* galvanized support for independence by the sheer audacity, flair, and novelty of Paine's rhetoric. Paine was an itinerant English radical who had arrived in Philadelphia in 1774. He dismissed monarchy and all hereditary privilege as artificial and immoral. He claimed that Americans possessed ample resources to defeat Britain on the battlefield, and he identified the lingering desire for last-minute reconciliation, for delay, for caution as the central impediment to the realization of American adulthood. The sensational response to *Common Sense* put advocates of delay and caution hopelessly on the defensive. On April 12, 1776 the North Carolina Provincial Congress authorized its delegates to the Continental Congress to vote for independence, and on May 15 the Virginia Convention positively endorsed a resolution that the United Colonies "are and of right ought to be free and independent States." On June 11 Congress appointed a committee to draft a declaration of independence. With Thomas Jefferson as its chief author, the Declaration was approved by Congress on July 2 and formally adopted on July 4, 1776.

How and why did it happen? What combination of forces and circumstances ignited a revolution for national independence? The answer is twofold: ideology and technique were the essential preconditions.

THE IDEOLOGY OF RESISTANCE

The term "ideology" is not an attractive one to many people because it implies the grim mind-set of extremists so scarred by their sense of outrage that they are driven to embrace a rigid view of social and political morality. The negative connotation has recently begun to give way to a more sympathetic view of ideology as any cluster of assumptions, beliefs, hopes, and fears that exerts an explanatory force over current events sufficiently compelling to thrust men into political action. Such an approach is essential to understanding politics in eighteenth-century America—a cultural setting charged with all sorts of unfulfilled expectations and permeated with new ideas about society, institutions, and the human spirit. The making of a revolutionary ideology occurred in several distinct stages: a variety of seventeenth- and eighteenth-century ideas crossed the Atlantic and became implanted in people's minds; because these ideas dealt with, among other things, questions of power, social virtue, and public morality, they had an unexpected appeal to colonial leaders caught up in controversy with Britain about taxes and imperial administration; finally, the use of these ideas as weapons against British measures was so unrehearsed and spontaneous that Americans suddenly discovered that they were a unique people for whom republican government was a natural and desirable goal. That vital intellectual and emotional experience occurred in several different spheres, which, for convenience, may be labeled *legislative, polemical, religious,* and *provincial.*

The colonial legislatures played a central but easily misunderstood role in the making of revolutionary ideology. The assemblies were not seeds of democracy destined in some inevitable fashion to transform American politics, nor were they especially virtuous, capable, or wise. But the assemblies were extremely important educational centers—places where people could learn about power, the interests of the community, and collective action. Assemblymen became acutely aware of the power of precedent. Once an assembly secured the power to tax, control the militia, regulate the Anglican Church in colonies where it was established, audit the colony's books, make executive appointments, or establish courts and units of local government, it regarded that function as its perpetual and exclusive preserve. This concern for precedent and the scrutiny of past legislative records in search of precedent was not a systematic or conscious attempt to garner power. The assemblies did not have a long-range goal of legislative domination. They were simply acting defensively, holding on to what had been gained in the past, and concerned lest royal governors acting at the behest of the bureaucracy in London should sweep away all the autonomy and shared responsibility that the assemblies had won over the years. The assemblies were preoccupied with specific constituent pressures to regulate the economy, maintain an adequate money supply, defend the colony against Indian or French or Spanish adversaries, keep the criminal and civil law up-to-date, respect the interests of dominant political families, and keep royal governors and Crown officials from running roughshod over local sentiments. Before 1763 or 1764 these tasks left assemblymen with little time to reflect on the long-term constitutional position of the assemblies; after news of the Grenville program reached America, all of their specific functions seemed inperiled.

Buried in the routine proceedings of the assemblies and also broadcast in their dramatic clashes with imperial authority was an implicit, comprehensive rationale for government by consent of the governed. The assemblies modeled themselves on the House of Commons and drew inspiration from the seventeenth-century struggles between Parliament and the Crown. As we saw in Chapter 1, they discovered in that history two rival interpretations of the nature of politics: the notion that the Crown itself was a vital center of energy and wisdom (the doctrine of will) and the contrary view that the Crown possessed only those powers that experience and tradition had allowed it to exercise (the doctrine of custom). Following the Revolution of 1688, the conflict between those two doctrines seemed to evaporate; the Crown no longer claimed supremacy, and Parliament, which had won *its* supremacy, no longer needed to remind the king that he was not a power

60

unto himself. The King, Lords, and Commons now seemed to represent the basic elements of the social order, and political stability depended on integrating the three orders into the institutions of government.

But the colonial assemblies continued to cherish the distinction. They saw themselves as a bulwark between their constituents and arbitrary royal authority. The assemblies chose the term "the public good" to describe the interests, welfare, and security of their constituents, and they insisted that only the representatives of the people were entitled to make authoritative statements about the public good. Underlying these presumptions were the most deeply rooted of all colonial political ideas: the belief that government rested on a compact between ruler and ruled and the corollary belief that the sinful nature of human beings made both the ruler and the subject susceptible to antisocial behavior. The central problem of politics, then, was to find ways to induce sinful subjects and rulers to restrain their passions—to achieve a kind of implicit non-aggression pact under which the ruled would be obedient, cooperative, and constructive and the ruler would be wise, self-sacrificing, and well-mannered.

The assemblies rarely had an opportunity to enunciate these beliefs in a systematic way. Perhaps for that reason, English philosopher John Locke's powerful and cogent analysis of these issues in his *Two Treatises on Government* (1689) filled a vacuum in colonial thought. Few colonists understood the subtleties of Locke's writing, but he had a genius for simplifying his arguments so that the *Two Treatises* served the needs of a broad spectrum of readers. At the simplest level Locke restated a basic tenet of seventeenth-century Parliamentary thought: that society rests on a compact between ruler and ruled. Locke stressed that the compact was a voluntary agreement between equals. If the ruler grossly violated his duty and destroyed the liberty of his subjects, they had a right and an obligation to establish a new government. On a more complex level Locke was also arguing that human beings were insecure, fragile creatures. The knowledge that their property and persons were secure from arbitrary seizure or violence was essen-

26 John Locke.

tial to transform them from cowed and intimidated (or violent a
rebellious) victims of oppression into responsible free people. T
location of power was the crucial element in maintaining a stal
and uncoerced political system. If power descended from God
the king and from the king to individuals, as some roya
theorists maintained, then people would always feel insecure a
unable to trust their own reason. But if power resided in the co
pact itself, from whence it spread outward to the ruler and the su
jects, people would feel free of fear and resentment and willing
trust their own reason. Locke powerfully reinforced and elaborat
the assemblies' assumptions about the nature of politics.

The second factor influencing the creation of a revolutiona
ideology in the colonies was the development of a new kind of p
lemical writing that altered the whole political atmosphere and

directed the behavior of colonial politicians. These new writings were based on a body of ideas known as the "Country ideology," which was an approach to politics fashioned by opposition political theorists in England from the 1690s through the 1730s. These writers were highly educated and resourceful men who had been excluded from public life by the fierce jealousies and animosities of the age. Distinguishing themselves from the "Court party" of ministerial, royal, and Parliamentary insiders, the Country party theorists proclaimed that the integrity of the individual transcended the claims of parties and institutions. The Country party condemned the tendency of factions and governments to corrupt the integrity of the individual; it saw the power of government as an amoral and potentially destructive force; it celebrated the virtue and benevolence of the unfettered, property-owning individual but at the same time agonized over the frailty of humanity and the ease with which ignorance, greed, bigotry, complacency, or vanity seduced people's civic responsibility. These idealistic beliefs were relatively harmless in England and hence their publication was tolerated. But in the colonies these depictions of power and individualism were enormously attractive.

The Country ideology was appealing in part because it took the form of a history of English liberty that surveyed the subtle, sinister tactics used by kings and courtiers to usurp power from the people and from Parliament and described the rise of religious toleration for Protestants. Distinguishing themselves from the powerful Whig factions of the early eighteenth century, the historians of the Country ideology called themselves "real Whigs," meaning that they, and not the powerful politicians, were the guardians of individual liberty and conscience. The earliest and most influential was Viscount Robert Molesworth, an Anglo-Irish nobleman and Protestant who fled to Denmark during the reign of James II and returned there as a diplomatic envoy following the Revolution of 1688. There he wrote *An Account of Denmark as It Was in the Year 1692*. Ostensibly an account of the death of liberty in Denmark, it was really an indictment of England's failure to reform its institutions following the Revolution of 1688. The Danes, like the

English, allowed a standing army in time of peace, permitted royal power to influence the conduct of Parliament, tolerated an oppressive established church, and were betrayed by an aristocracy that would not resist the ambitions of the king. Molesworth's *Account of Denmark* became the original scripture of the Country ideology, and it anticipated the grievances that an articulate though ineffectual minority of Englishmen would feel in the early eighteenth century. From within the Church of England itself Bishop Benjamin Hoadly repudiated the established Church's claim to moral or spiritual authority. During the 1720s and 1730s John Trenchard and Thomas Gordon published a series of writings under the titles *Cato's Letters* and *The Independent Whig*, which berated high-church Anglicans and Catholics alike, condemned the greed and arrogance of Robert Walpole's government, and, using classical and seventeenth-century English historical examples, emphasized that only balanced government, in which power was widely dispersed among many groups, could be trusted to avoid oppression and that royal and ministerial corruption was the chief threat to that balance. The exiled French Huguenot historian, Paul de Rapin-Thoyras, wrote a *Dissertation on the . . . Whigs and Tories* (1717) and a longer *History of England* (1725–1731), which popularized the notion that Saxon England, prior to the Norman conquest, had been a free and open society and that ever since 1066 English history had been blighted by authoritarianism and privilege. On the eve of the American Revolution, James Burgh, an obscure Scottish schoolmaster, in *Political Disquisitions* (1774) brought the ideas of the Country ideology to bear on the problems of the reign of George III. Burgh denounced the unrepresentative nature of the House of Commons, saw in policies of recent ministries a conspiracy to subvert English liberty, and championed the cause of the American colonies. This band of historians, from Molesworth to Burgh, were widely read and quoted in the colonies and reinforced the predisposition of educated colonists to think of politics as a constant struggle between good and evil and to search continually for the location of power and the available restraints against its abuse.

As a detailed examination of the behavior of individual ministers and officials and a blueprint for the vigilant defense of liberty, the Country ideology heightened interest in the study of the human mind and personality. The most advanced work in these areas during the eighteenth century was done by a cluster of Scottish theorists known as the Scottish Common Sense school of philosophy, of which the central figure was Francis Hutcheson. Scottish and American intellectuals had an affinity for each other. Contacts between the two regions increased throughout the century, and both shared a sense of being cultural provinces of England, insecure in the presence of the London metropolis. The Common Sense philosophers were a part of the Enlightenment, a movement in western thought during the eighteenth century that stressed human reason and the liberation of the human spirit. In contrast with most Enlightenment thinkers, who trusted only concrete facts about human behavior, Hutcheson believed that the mind contained innate moral potentialities of benevolence, sociability, and civil responsibility, which education and moral instruction could awaken and activate. He taught that politics, even violent resistance against unjust government, was a potentially ennobling experience. Through the writings of two prominent Scottish emigrants to the colonies, James Wilson, a Pennsylvania lawyer, and John Witherspoon, President of the College of New Jersey (Princeton), the Common Sense philosophy added an element of sophistication, assurance, and daring to pre-Revolutionary ideology.

A third key to the development of that ideology lies in colonial religious thought. More than any other single factor, religion preconditioned colonial Americans to take human nature seriously and to regard politics as a moral saga. The Great Awakening of 1739–1740, a tumultuous evangelical movement that spread throughout the colonies among rich and poor alike, revealed a crisis of authority in American society. For more than a century the Congregationalist clergy in New England—as well as Dutch Reformed and Presbyterian clergy in the middle colonies—had occupied a special place of status and influence in the community. During the early decades of the eighteenth century that influence had become formal and brittle. The established families of the social elite often dominated community life and made churches into respectable, stabilizing institutions. But an increasingly large segment of the population was outside of the reach of the church, and as population increased and the economy expanded, an accompanying rise in crime, sexual offenses, quarrels over property and money, and physical violence created the impression that the old values of religion, piety, obedience to authority, and respect for a moral code were about to disappear. Alarmed by the declining influence of the church and at the same time seeking to please a conservative and privileged laity, many clergy became rationalist in their theology and preaching—that is, they stressed the rationalist ideas that people were not innately evil, that good works were an intrinsic part of achieving salvation, and that a benevolent God bestowed on people the freedom to choose to live in a state of grace. The Great Awakening was a rebellion against both the rationalist theology and the established church organizations. It insisted that people were thoroughly sinful, capricious, self-destructive, and self-deluding and that only a cleansing and purging experience of salvation could cut through the crust of complacency.

The towering figure of the Awakening, the Reverend Jonathan Edwards of Northampton, Massachusetts, fashioned from these religious beliefs a critique of American society itself. Edwards was the first colonial intellectual to take seriously Locke's teaching that the human mind contained no innate ideas and that all knowledge, including divine inspiration, came through the senses. This psychological insight, Edwards argued, required that preaching depict damnation and salvation in vivid sensuous terms: the heat, glow, fiery roar, sulfurous odors, and shrieks of the damned in Hell and the sweet, soothing, melodious, embracing sensations of salvation. Only in this way could the leaders of society reestablish communication with the people and fulfill their divine obligation to give their fellow human beings moral leadership. Edwards was aware that this kind of preaching would offend many people. It split churches and communities to their very foundations. The

27 Jonathan Edwards.

Congregationalists broke into New Light and Old Light factions, Presbyterians into New Side and Old Side, and Dutch Reformed into the Coetus faction, which was anxious to Americanize the church, and the Conferentie faction, which retained its ties to the parent church in Holland and resisted all innovations in worship and theology. In Connecticut New Light and Old Light political factions battled for political power.

Both evangelical advocates of revivalism and their rationalist critics played leading roles in the mobilization of resistance against British encroachments. By breaking down the isolation of the clergy and by making theological disputation a central part of community life, the Awakening drew clergymen of all persuasions more directly into political life. The evangelicals believed that ecstatic revival would fuse the people of America into a new fellowship of pious, joyful, self-disciplined, self-sacrificing, and democratic beings; in this way they defined colonial identity in moral and spiritual terms a generation before the Revolution would de-

S I N N E R S

In the Hands of an

Angry GOD.

A S E R M O N

Preached at *Enfield*, *July* 8th 1 7 4 1.

At a Time of great Awakenings ; and attended with remarkable Impreffions on many of the Hearers.

By *Jonathan Edwards*, A.M.

Paftor of the Church of CHRIST in *Northampton*.

Amos ix. 2, 3. *Though they dig into Hell, thence fhall mine Hand take them ; though they climb up to Heaven, thence will I bring them down. And though they bide themfelves in the Top of Carmel, I will fearch and take them out thence ; and though they be hid from my Sight in the Bottom of the Sea, thence I will command the Serpent, and he fhall bite them.*

B O S T O N: Printed and Sold by S. KNEELAND and T. GREEN. in Queen-Street over againft the Prifon, 1 7 4 1.

28   Title page of a sermon by Jonathan Edwards.

fine it in political and constitutional language. They considered the defeat of Catholic France in the Seven Years' War a sign of God's protection and an indication that He would postpone a little longer time of judgment and retribution.[2] After 1764 they saw British encroachments as a warning that God's patience was wearing thin. But only the penitent, they predicted, could expect divine help in struggle against tyranny.

Rationalist clergy, who were uncomfortable with this appeal to feeling and emotional experience, were no less apprehensive about British policies in the 1760s and early 1770s. Religious as well as civil liberty seemed to them in jeopardy. Rationalist Congregationalists and Presbyterians in the middle colonies focused their a tacks on the Anglican Church and created a firestorm of protest against Anglican proposals for the appointment of an American bishop. The British government had no intention of permitting the establishment of an American episcopate, but the clamorous demands by a clique of high Anglican clergy in New Jersey, New York, and Connecticut for a bishop in America provoked corrosive religious disputes and spread alarm about British intentions throughout the region. The most controversial feature of Anglicanism was its teaching of passive submission to those in political authority; in condemning that doctrine, the rationalists were forced to support the converse of passive submission—the positive duty of Christians to resist tyranny and to protect the blessings of political liberty that God bestowed upon His people. Traditionally, New England Congregationalists had emphasized that the compact between the magistrate and the subject was a religious concept and that both parties to the compact had an obligation to God to behave with responsibility and restraint. While warning against the dangers of precipitate resistance and uncontrolled violence, the rationalist clergy conceded that in the last resort and with the support of the whole community colonists might conceivably be justified in using force to preserve their liberty. Cautious and conservative, the rationalists reflected the sentiments of many—perhaps a majority—of their parishioners, and in the process they greatly expanded the base of the pre-Revolutionary movement.

The most pointed and explicit religious component of revolutionary ideology was the Puritan ethic, the characteristically American belief that every person receives a divine calling to do a particular work in the world and to practice thrift, prudence, self-control, and craftsmanship in the stewardship of his or her talents and wealth. The Great Awakening altered the function and structure of the Puritan ethic. By freeing people from anxiety about their salvation and from the belief that good works were a precondition to eternal life, the Awakening appealed to newly rich merchants and landowners. The well-to-do who had experienced salvation did not need to regret their wealth; moreover, their emotional vitality—newly heightened by their salvation—was just as much a gift of God as their property and talents. By emphasizing these aspects of experience, the Awakening unshackled the acquisitiveness of its converts. The Awakening did not condone materialism; rather it stressed that people's emotions and self-consciousness were gifts to be used with the same responsibility and strictness that the older version of the ethic applied to material possessions. When the colonists imposed nonimportation boycotts on British goods during the crises following the Stamp Act, Townshend duties, and Coercive Acts, many patriots argued that self-denial would purge society of complacency, selfishness, and other sins unworthy of a free people. "We may talk and boast of liberty," declared a writer called "Frugality" in 1774, "but, after all, only the industrious and frugal will be free."[3] When the Reverend David Caldwell rallied his Guilford County, North Carolina parishioners to support the Revolutionary cause in 1775, he entitled his sermon "The Character and Doom of the Sluggard" and decried the tendency of moral, political, and personal slothfulness to paralyze the people's spirit in time of public and religious crisis.[4]

Underlying all of these changes in political belief and attitude that developed in the areas of legislative activity, polemical writing, and religious thought was the unsettling condition of provincialism. Prosperity and social stability gave the colonists a heady sense of their own capability, but they could not ignore the reality that they lived on the periphery of the Empire and that their lives were affected in many ways by events in London over which they had little control. To bolster their confidence they claimed the rights of Britons and asserted that they were valuable participants in the life of the Empire. Yet the mother country from whence their rights and prosperity came was rapidly changing in disturbing and confusing ways. Provincialism and remoteness from Britain made the colonists conscious of their uniqueness, but it also undermined their confidence and security. Colonial culture was in disequilibrium.

The most important change in the colonists' perception of Britain was the growing conviction during the decade following the Stamp Act crisis that there was a ministerial and bureaucratic conspiracy to subvert colonial liberty and impose imperial despotism in its place. John Dickinson's writings throughout the 1760s identified a pattern of British encroachments in the Stamp Act, Declaratory Act, Townshend duties, Quartering Act, tightened vice-admiralty jurisdiction, and changes in judicial tenure. Far from being coincidental, these policies must have sprung from a hidden, sinister decision at the highest levels of imperial administration. Behind this pattern Dickinson perceived an insatiable appetite for power and dominion; its symptoms were ambition, secrecy, bureaucratic hauteur, and an attitude of superiority. Taken together, these manifestations of humanity's sinful nature indicated that British officialdom had sunk into a morass of wickedness. They could not be reasoned with nor dissuaded by appeals to conscience or tradition. The colonists would have to rouse themselves to vigilance and discipline and counteract evil ministerial designs by persistent and restrained opposition to British policies. The strongest evidence that an amoral, irrational conspiracy gripped the British government was the damage that had already been done to the British constitution. In place of its traditional balance, stability, and concern for the liberties of the subject was a new political system in which evil counsellors misled the king and the supporters of colonial liberty in Parliament were an ineffectual minority. "A series of occurrences, many recent events," declared the Boston Town Meeting in 1770, "afford great reason to believe that a deep-laid and desperate plan of imperial despotism has been laid and partly executed for the extinction of all civil liberty. . . . The august and once revered fortress of English freedom—the admirable work of ages—the BRITISH CONSTITUTION seems fast tottering into fatal and inevitable ruin."[5]

The most dramatic evidence of conspiracy was the sensational career of John Wilkes, a somewhat dissolute and opportunistic radical critic of the British political establishment during the 1760s and 1770s. He had attacked the ministry in a publication called the *North Briton Number 45* (1763) and the administration had pushed through Parliament a general warrant for his arrest. Wilkes fled to France and returned to England in 1767 to run for Parliament.

29 John Wilkes in an etching by William Hogarth.

Elected to the House of Commons, expelled at the express desire of the king, and then sent to jail on the old charges that *North Briton 45* was libelous and that his *Essay on Woman* (1763) was obscene, Wilkes on returning to London touched off serious mob violence there in protest to his treatment. Thus Wilkes brought into the open widespread radical disenchantment with the political leadership of the day. Nearly a quarter of the qualified voters in the kingdom signed petitions asking Parliament to allow Wilkes to take his seat. He also had aristocratic supporters who provided financial backing and formed the Society of Gentlemen Supporters of the Bill of Rights to advance his cause.

Colonial newspapers followed Wilkes' career closely. Colonial political activists noted that Wilkes was steeped in the writings of the Country ideology. They compared the general warrant used against him with the similarly highhanded writs of assistance employed by Boston customs officials against merchants suspected of smuggling. Wilkes corresponded with colonial admirers, and Dickinson's *Letters of a Pennsylvania Farmer* apparently convinced him that restrained and tempered radical protest was more potent than mere uninhibited exhibitionism by unruly crowds such as those who had demonstrated upon his return to London. While Wilkes languished in prison in 1769, an enormous protest movement in his behalf led by an Anglican vicar, the Reverend John Horne Tooke, played on Wilkes's martyrdom and kept the City of Westminster in upheaval. Colonial rights, reform of English rule in Ireland, and extension of the voting franchise in Britain became themes of the movement for "Wilkes and Liberty." Released from prison in 1770, Wilkes remained a popular figure and finally became Lord Mayor of London. But he lacked the doggedness and zeal necessary for the leader of a continuing mass movement. A protest symbol rather than a practical politician, Wilkes nonetheless had a significant impact on the coming of the Revolution in America. He provided a vivid example of moral protest against British ministerial power in 1768 and 1769, a period when colonial leaders were groping for a means of sustaining their opposition to the Townshend program. Even his ultimate ineffectiveness may have convinced his strongest admirers that British government policy could not be modified even in the face of an outraged populace.

An amalgam of diverse traditions, ideas, and preoccupations, the ideology of resistance quietly coalesced during the early 1770s into a unified faith and sense of determination. A key to that elusive process was the colonists' resurrection in the late 1760s and early 1770s of the labels "Whig" and "Tory" to describe the contending sides in the pre-Revolutionary debate. The term "Tory" became an ugly epithet hurled at Crown officeholders and supporters of British authority. In English history the Whigs had demanded and the Tories had opposed the exclusion of the Duke of York from the throne in 1680–1683 (though the Tories quietly acquiesced in his overthrow in 1688); until 1713 the Whigs had supported war against France, toleration for dissenters, and the Hanoverian succession to the throne against varying degrees of Tory opposition. A few Tories in 1714 conspired to prevent the Hanoverian ruler from becoming King George I by seeking the restoration of the Stuart pretender, James III; their failure discredited all Tories, and by the 1720s they had ceased to be a serious opposition force, though a handful of obstreperous political figures continued to call themselves Tories.

The terms Whig and Tory were therefore inapplicable to pre-Revolutionary American politics. Ruling ministers in Britain were—along with the overwhelming majority of Parliament—Whigs of one sort or another and considered themselves champions of Parliamentary supremacy, the legacy of the Revolution of 1688. The future loyalists—men and women so closely identified with the Crown that they were bound by interest and inclination to support British authority—held beliefs that were much closer to the Whig than the Tory tradition. They nearly all believed in government by consent and in extreme cases the right of resistance. Moreover, most of them had serious misgivings about the justice and wisdom of British encroachments on colonial liberty.

Yet at a deeper level the terms Whig and Tory were valid and penetrating ways of describing political reality. A crisis of unknown dimensions and consequences did seem imminent, and if it occurred, Tories were those likely to prefer continued submission to the risks of violent resistance. By using the term Whig to describe themselves, patriot leaders could reassure hesitant followers by associating themselves with the "real Whigs" of the Country ideology and with a moderate defense of law and liberty that English Whigs had generally supported since the 1680s. Although they did not adopt the term until they began establishing new governments in early 1776, the Whigs were really becoming republicans. Crudely defined, republicanism meant a social and political order devoid of hereditary privilege and monarchy. But the term was rich with other implications when the Whigs first began to use it in 1775 and 1776. Republicanism, writes Bernard Bailyn, meant a society "where authority was distrusted and held in constant scrutiny; where the status of men flowed from their achievements and from their personal qualities, not from distinctions ascribed to them at birth; and where the use of power over the lives of men was jealously guarded and severely restricted."[6]

THE TECHNIQUES OF RESISTANCE

Ideology did not cause Americans to resist British authority, but it did instill into the people a new sense of urgency, loosen restraints on political activism, and help to legitimize new forms of protest. It is probably fair to conclude that ideology so accelerated the pace of events and charged the political atmosphere that without it the Revolution would not have occurred in anything resembling the form it took in 1774 to 1776. The movement of resistance, however, did not sustain itself spontaneously. It required a great deal of work and effort. The tactics that Whig leaders employed were not a conscious attempt to achieve independence—although Crown officials and their colonial allies accused the Whigs of throwing off all subjection to British authority. No one seriously contemplated independence until late 1775, when it became clear that Britain was going to use military force in America. Instead, Whig tactics were a deliberate effort to create a structure of resistance and remonstrance that would protect communities and colonies from British coercion.

As a result of these defensive steps, there was an erosion of British power in much of New England and in major port towns before 1774 and almost everywhere in 1774 to 1776. This step-by-step assumption of power by popular leaders required broad public support and the use of tactics that were manifestly moderate and defensive. In order to proceed "without mobs or riots," the Petersham, Massachusetts, Committee of Correspondence resolved in April 1773, "the people of this province" must "resume the liberties enjoyed under their old charter and choose all our officers." Because existing royal officials were implicated in the attack on the colony's liberty, they could not be trusted to reclaim the colony's rights; "it must be done by the common people." In order to avoid violence, there must be a seizure of power by the people themselves—that was the formula for resistance that evolved from the conflicts of the pre-Revolutionary period. American resistance was then a vital symbiosis, or joining, of radical and conservative tactics and principles.

The cutting edge of resistance was the emergence of the mob as a direct response to British actions. Mob violence had long been a recurrent part of colonial life. Mob action was often a positive attempt by the community to solve problems that local or colonial governments were unwilling or unable to resolve. During an outbreak of crime in the South Carolina back country in 1767–1768—when the assembly in Charles Town could not provide enough courts and sheriffs to handle the problem in the area—prominent landowners formed vigilante mobs who rounded up suspected outlaws and inflicted brutal corporal punishment. In Pennsylvania in 1764 and North Carolina in 1771 angry farmers rose in brief rebellion against the practices of their respective assemblies, which were dominated by eastern interests. In northern port towns gangs of seamen banded together to resist impressment into the British navy, and their courage won the sympathy of juries, who refused to convict rioting sailors, and of lawyers like John Adams, who in one case successfully argued that the killing of a British naval officer by a seaman resisting illegal impressment was justifiable homicide. Tenant farmers in New Jersey in 1747 and in Dutchess County, New York, in 1766 rioted against oppressive landlords. Successful mobs had their own internal leadership and sought to secure specific objectives. Although they often drew members from various levels of the social scale—especially skilled artisans—the sharp increase of urban poverty during the 1760s added more violent and volatile members to colonial mobs. However, prudent colonial leaders continued to believe that mobs were "symptoms of a strong and healthy constitution" and an integral check against oppressive or incompetent government. Without endorsing violence, colonial leaders institutionalized the mob and

30 A demonstration against the Stamp Act.

used it as a sharp reminder to British officials of the limits of American patience.

During the Stamp Act crisis the mobs were amazingly effective devices for attacking British power at its weakest points. The hapless colonists who accepted appointments as stamp distributors were beseiged by multitudes of angry demonstrators. Early in the morning of August 14, 1765, Massachusetts stamp distributor Andrew Oliver and former British minister Lord Bute were hanged in effigy in Boston. The council refused to condemn the action, and the sheriff declined to remove the effigies. That night a crowd carried the effigies through the streets and stopped at a partially completed building of Oliver's, which they wrecked to secure wood for a bonfire. The crowd then went to Oliver's house and, finding that he had fled the premises, broke into his wine cellar. When Oliver's kinsman, Lieutenant Governor Thomas Hutchinson, brought a sheriff to the scene to make arrests, the two men were driven away by a torrent of stones. The next day Oliver resigned his post as stamp distributor. But the memory of Hutchinson's attempted intervention perhaps still outraged the rioters, because on the night of August 26 a large crowd shouting "liberty and property" broke into the admiralty court and destroyed its records, then vandalized the home of Customs Commissioner Benjamin Hallowell, and finally demolished the interior of Hutchinson's mansion —breaking down doors and smashing windows, ripping apart bedding, destroying crystal and portraits, throwing Hutchinson's books and manuscripts into the muddy street, and making off with the family silver and a large sum of cash. The Reverend Jonathan Mayhew, who had advocated demonstrations against the Stamp Act a few days earlier, was shocked at the way a drunken and frenzied mob had got out of hand, and he apologized to the lieutenant governor.

News of the attacks on Oliver's and Hutchinson's houses spread throughout the colonies and placed every stamp distributor in jeopardy. Distributors in New Hampshire, New Jersey, and New York resigned immediately. In Rhode Island two leading defenders of British authority, Martin Howard and Thomas Moffat, defied the mobs who then hanged them in effigy. After Moffat's and Howard's homes in Newport were sacked, however, their friend, stamp distributor Augustus Johnston, resigned his post. In Connecticut stamp distributor Jared Ingersoll, who was one of the most respected men in the colony, ignored the many towns that hanged him in effigy and set out for Hartford to defend his acceptance of his post before the assembly. A large crowd intercepted him at Wethersfield, and after they had subjected him to three hours of argument and threats, he wearily agreed to resign and even to throw his hat into the air as the crowd cheered for "liberty and property."

Alarmed by news of violence in other colonies, New York Lieutenant Governor Cadwallader Colden asked General Gage for troops to keep order in New York City when the stamps arrived. Gage had no troops to spare and told Colden to make do with the small garrison stationed in Fort George on the southern tip of Manhattan. When the stamps arrived on a British warship, Colden made ostentatious preparations to store them in the fort. Fearful of using British troops against the populace, Gage pointedly warned Colden that his men would not fire on rioters unless ordered to do so by the civil officials. On November 1, 1765 an enormous crowd gathered outside the fort, sacked the house of one particularly obnoxious officer, hanged Colden in effigy, and demanded the surrender of the stamps. Gage insisted that Colden surrender the stamps, and they were turned over to the city government for safe keeping. Only in Georgia, where Governor James Wright had troops under his personal control, was the Stamp Act enforced and stamps used according to law. Everywhere else, mob violence or the threat of direct attacks on the stamp distributors or of confiscation of the stamps themselves prevented enforcement.

31 Lieutenant Governor Cadwallader Colden of New York.

The task of coordinating and directing protest and resistance against the Stamp Act fell to informal groups of men who took the name "Sons of Liberty"—a phrase used by Colonel Isaac Barre in a speech to the House of Commons denouncing the Stamp Act and praising the colonists for their resistance. Made up of lawyers and merchants as well as skilled artisans and tradesmen, the Sons of Liberty were men of property and standing, with intimate knowledge of the politics and economic life of their communities and the capacity to organize demonstrations, print timely broadsides, indulge in oratory, and select the tactics necessary to prevent enforcement of the Stamp Act. While these groups did not continue to function as organizations after the Stamp Act crisis was over, the leading members of the Sons of Liberty kept in contact with each other and established a network of communication throughout the colonies. The presence of organized, vigilant, active groups of men constantly keeping alive the discussion of grievances and resistance had a subtle but profoundly destabilizing effect on the politics of several colonies.

In New York the Sons of Liberty were led by three men, Alexander McDougall, Isaac Sears, and John Lamb. They were self-made merchants who had risen from the level of tradesmen by luck, hard work, and sharp tactics. They never achieved political power in their own right, but their activities and popularity upset delicate balances between factions and interest groups in the colony in a way that brought New York into a state of rebellion. New York politics had been dominated since the 1730s by rival factions led by the Livingston and De Lancey families. The Presbyterian Livingstons had traditionally espoused libertarian ideas, especially religious toleration, though they were a more loosely knit and informal group than the Anglican De Lanceys, who had been until the late 1750s the masters of Anglo-American politics working through a network of highly placed agents in the British establishment. Both factions saw politics as a means of acquiring land, offices, favorable treatment in the courts, and laws beneficial to their interests; both were alarmed by British encroachments in the 1760s and prepared to defend the colony's liberty. The Livingstons and De Lanceys were also willing to use the pre-Revolutionary

32   Estate of Henry Livingston at Poughkeepsie, ca. 1790.

controversy for partisan gain, each by depicting the other as a British lackey or a half-hearted friend of colonial liberty. Both factions saw in the Sons of Liberty and in the volatile lower class of New York City a useful source of political support that they rather naively believed they could manipulate. When the Massachusetts circular letter condemning the Townshend duties reached the New York assembly in the autumn of 1768, the Livingston majority declined to act on it. Only a year earlier the assembly had been suspended by Parliament for failing to comply fully with terms of the Quartering Act. The Livingston members knew that Hillsborough had ordered royal governors to prorogue assemblies that tried to discuss the Massachusetts message. Rather than throw away all the advantages of controlling the legislature, they decided to move cautiously. The De Lanceys then saw their chance to regain power. They forced consideration of the Massachusetts circular letter, denounced the Livingstons for complying with the Quartering Act, associated the Livingstons with the Townshend duties, forced the governor to dissolve the assembly and call for a new election, and then won a smashing electoral triumph.

33 Alexander McDougall, leader of the New York Sons of Liberty.

Once in power, the De Lanceys set about reinforcing their position by making an alliance with Lieutenant Governor Cadwallader Colden, who was serving as acting governor until a newly appointed royal governor arrived. Colden had spent half a century in New York politics as a royal official and advocate of strong British administration of the colony. He hated the colonial aristocracy and detested their political and social power; he was as much an adversary of the De Lanceys as of the Livingstons. By an alliance with their old enemy, the De Lanceys could silence a critic who still had influence in the British bureaucracy; and Colden, on his part, would gain financial compensation for damage done to his property during the Stamp Act riots. The Livingstons countered by luring Lamb and Sears, two leaders of the Sons of Liberty who had previously been De Lancey men, into a new alliance. The Livingstons covertly encouraged the newly united trio of McDougall (who was already a Livingston man), Sears, and Lamb to unleash a barrage of personal criticism against Colden and the De Lanceys. The presence of British troops in New York—which was headquarters for the British army in North America—provided an opening. As the Livingstons had done, in 1767–1768 when they were in power, the De Lanceys complied with the Quartering Act. Insults and abuse directed at British soldiers became a way of embarrassing the De Lanceys and Colden. The radicals erected a liberty pole, and individual British soldiers who took offense cut it down. In January 1770 there were several pitched battles between club-swinging crowds and British troops. In this atmosphere, Alexander McDougall wrote an anonymous broadside, "To the Betrayed Inhabitants of the City and Colony of New York," accusing Colden, the De Lanceys, and the Crown of a corrupt deal by which Colden would receive his salary, his children holding Crown jobs would be secure from dismissal, and the De Lancey-controlled assembly would vote funds for the support of the army in the colony. Identified as the author, McDougall was arrested for seditious libel. He refused bail and spent eighty-one days in jail. Visited there by scores of admirers and proclaimed an American Wilkes (Wilkes' own imprisonment for seditious libel lasted until April 1770), McDougall became a public hero.

With the collapse of nonimportation in 1770 and a backlash in New York against political disorder, the Sons of Liberty seemed to decline as a political force. But their alliance with the Livingstons remained intact, and they stayed in close touch with leaders in Boston. In December 1773 they were instrumental in mobilizing crowds protesting the Tea Act, and they prevented the importation of the newly taxed tea into New York City. In May 1774 when Boston appealed to New York for common action to oppose the Coercive Acts, the New York Sons of Liberty again used their skill as organizers of public protest to frighten the De Lancey faction into creating a committee of fifty-one members to respond to Boston. Outvoted and outmaneuvered on the committee itself, the Sons of Liberty were able to force a compromise in which New York supported the idea of a general congress and elected a moderate delegation representing Livingston as well as De Lancey interests.

In Massachusetts the Boston Committee of Correspondence played an even more effective role in shifting the balance of political power against the Crown at a critical time. When Thomas Hutchinson became royal governor in 1771—after serving as lieutenant governor under Francis Bernard in the 1760s and as acting governor since 1769—he doubted whether he had the political strength to restore tranquility to Massachusetts. He did not underestimate, however, his major political asset: his political influence in towns outside of Boston. Through the careful use of political patronage and the nurturing of lifelong friendships, Hutchinson knew he could count on many towns to oppose the extremism of Boston. The Boston Committee of Correspondence was created by the Boston Town Meeting in 1772 to act as a continuous link between the capital and the towns of the colony. Unlike committees of correspondence within the lower house of the assembly, which could meet only when the assembly was in session, the Boston committee could meet continually. Unlike the Town Meeting, which was a cumbersome public assembly, it could do its work informally and efficiently. The committee did much more than write letters; it collected intelligence, planned strategy, polished arguments and public appeals, and maintained a network of communication with other Massachusetts towns. Its twenty-one members included several wealthy merchants, lawyers, and physicians, all with local political experience and high social rank. Samuel Adams, one of Boston's four representatives to the assembly, was a member, but the other three Boston representatives declined to serve. The committee's first assignment from the Town Meeting was to draft a comprehensive statement of Massachusetts' grievances, to be distributed in pamphlet form throughout the colony. Entitled *The Votes and Proceedings of the Freeholders and Other Inhabitants of Boston*, it was a new kind of protest literature. Aimed at a Massachusetts audience, it sought to analyze the whole welter of events in the colony during the preceding seven years: the Declaratory Act, new customs commissioners, British troops in Boston, independent Crown salaries for the governor and judges, tightened vice-admiralty controls, the threat of an American Angli-

34   A New England town meeting held in a Congregational church.

35 Samuel Adams, Massachusetts polemicist and tactician.

can bishop. It also contained a statement on the natural rights of man asserting the familiar doctrine that government rested on a compact and that the only permissible deprivations of individual freedom were ones "necessary for the great end of society, the best good of the whole." In its most striking phraseology, the *Votes and Proceedings* depicted government officials as "hired labourers" employed by and subordinate to the community. Parliament, moreover, did not and could not represent the interests of the colonists because that body was naturally inclined to pursue British interests to the sacrifice of the needs and welfare of all other people. Therefore, Parliament had no supreme authority over the colonists. The covering letter that accompanied the pamphlet observed that rumors of impending judicial salaries—which would make judges lackeys of the Crown, or independent of the passions of the community, depending on one's point of view—brought Massachusetts closer to the brink of despotism, and the committee asked the towns to ponder the problem. Rather than appear domineering, the Boston committee carefully avoided asking the towns to reply.[7]

Hutchinson at once recognized the disruptive consequences of allowing these sentiments to spread unchallenged. In a rare display of openness he called on the lower house and the council to repudiate the Boston *Votes and Proceedings*, and he offered to engage in an extended debate about the relationship of Massachusetts to the Empire. That debate was inconclusive but revealing. Hutchinson insisted that Parliamentary supremacy compelled the colonies to obey British law, and the house and council could only concede that Parliament had extensive but not unlimited authority over the colonies. To Hutchinson, the *Votes and Proceedings* were subversive not because they bandied about loose ideas about Parliamentary supremacy; rather they were dangerous because they provided a formal occasion for townspeople to meet and consider the nature of government. More than half of the 260 towns and districts of the colony formally replied to the Boston committee. The replies generally endorsed the view that Massachusetts had been assaulted by a succession of infringements on its liberty, but the towns did not simply echo the words of the Boston committee. They placed their own stamp on the discussion, emphasizing, for example, the "undoubted right to meet together . . . especially when an infringement is made upon their . . . liberties." The towns stressed repeatedly that resistance against tyranny was the positive duty of citizens and that oppression unresisted left its victims cowed, passive, and servile.

The establishment of a network of communication between the Boston Committee of Correspondence and the towns of the colony greatly increased the capacity of popular leaders to mobilize resistance. No longer did Boston have to feel it was standing alone, and no longer could Crown supporters infer from the relative tranquility of the countryside indifference about issues raised in Boston. In anticipation of the imminent arrival of tea shipped under the East India Company's new monopoly, a joint meeting of inhabitants of Boston, Roxbury, Dorchester, Brookline, and Cambridge attracted several thousand people to Boston on November 29, 1773. This meeting lasted, with periodical recesses, for two days. It extracted from Francis Rotch, owner of the first tea-bearing ship, a promise that the ship and its cargo would be returned to England, and it established the machinery for monitoring the arrival of suspicious ships. The consignees—who by this time had fled to Castle William, a British fort in Boston harbor—and the governor, however, refused to allow the return of the tea: the consignees on the ground that it was private property, and Hutchinson on the ground that once a ship entered the harbor he could not legally permit it to leave until all customs procedures were complied with and dutiable cargo unloaded. The Boston Committee of Correspondence then insisted that Rotch's tea-bearing ship, the *Dartmouth*, be brought to a wharf where it could be guarded by the committee. Throughout eastern Massachusetts town meetings gathered to protest against the entry of the tea into the colony. On the last day before the deadline for customs clearance, December 16, 1773, these committees staged a huge mass meeting in Boston. Representatives of this meeting made one last attempt to negotiate the removal of the tea from Boston. Hutchinson refused. A band of unidentified

36 A contemporary drawing of the Boston Tea Party showing a crowd of spectators.

men dressed as Indians then went aboard the *Dartmouth,* broke open the 342 chests of tea, and dumped the cargo into the harbor. When the Coercive Acts closed the port of Boston and suspended key provisions of the Massachusetts charter, the town meetings moved swiftly to take power into their own hands. Between July and September of 1774 the towns in ten of the colony's fifteen counties summoned county conventions. Although these conventions urged the need for calm and order, they were in the eyes of General Gage, the new royal governor, insurrectionary institutions because they claimed that ultimate authority rested with the people and called on the people to withhold obedience from royal officials appointed under the Massachusetts Government Act. Moving quickly to remove what they considered illegitimate power from the colony, crowds confronted all of the appointees to the new royal council and demanded resignation and repudiation of the Massachusetts Government Act. Eighteen of the thirty-seven new appointees to the council were outside of Boston when they learned of their appointment, and all eighteen were hounded into resignation. These men left, in written descriptions of their experience at the hands of the mob, an illuminating account of the nature of radicalism in Massachusetts. All were impressed by the broad cross section of the community represented in the crowds that forced them to resign; they noted the specific demands of the crowds—resignation and repudiation of the Massachusetts Government Act; they complied when they became convinced that violence would be used against them as a last resort. By the autumn of 1774 Gage's actual authority in Massachusetts did not extend beyond the boundaries of Boston.

The violence of the Boston populace and in much of the Massachusetts countryside, as well as the acumen and independence of elected officials, combined to destabilize Massachusetts politics. These factors weakened the capacity of Hutchinson and Gage to wait out periods of unrest. In contrast, in Philadelphia and New York civic and colonial leaders were deeply divided over the tactics and even propriety of resistance. In New York, as we have seen, the fortuitous alliance of Livingstons and Sons of Liberty combined to

37　Burns' Coffee House, New York City, meeting place of the Sons of Liberty.

weaken the fabric of acquiescence. In Philadelphia, the forces of radical resistance had no such powerful allies. Proprietary governor John Penn had no stake in the vindication of British authority, but he feared that continued instability would jeopardize the Penn family's interests. From 1765 to 1774 Quaker and Anglican leaders successfully supported moderate policies and sharply curtailed opposition to British measures. Extraconstitutional committees, created to enforce successive nonimportation boycotts, gradually became the instruments of radicalization and politicization. The 1765–1766 committee and its 1770 counterpart reflected the dominance of moderate, wealthy Quaker and Anglican merchants. A 1773 committee, organized to deal with the Tea Act crisis, contained a larger proportion of newly elected and younger members than the predecessor committees. Another committee, elected in June 1774, served as a rallying point for Pennsylvania's participation in a new continental congress. One elected the following November endorsed nonimportation and nonexportation, organized the city on a block-by-block basis, and included members of several religious and ethnic constituencies: Presbyterians, Lutherans, Scots, Scots-Irish, Welsh, and younger members of the Anglican and Quaker churches. German pietists, the traditional leaders of Anglican parishes, and the majority of strict pacifist Quakers abstained from involvement in the work of the November 1774 committee.

By the spring of 1776 Philadelphia moderates and radicals comprised coherent and well-organized parties. The moderates had the allegiance of a majority of the electorate. They appealed to a distinctive Philadelphia audience that yearned for accommodation with Britain, doubted whether either side in the imperial debate had a monopoly on the truth, and feared the havoc that revolution would cause to the colony's intricate economic and social system.[8] The radicals had the zeal of new converts to political action and the support of a majority of the colonies in the Continental Congress meeting in Philadelphia. The moderates won a majority in the May 1, 1776, assembly elections; the radicals then finessed the assembly by persuading Congress to resolve, by a margin of six colonies to four, that all governments deriving their authority from the Crown should be "totally suppressed." Backed by this congressional sanction, a mass meeting in Philadelphia on May 20, 1776, summoned a constitutional convention and denied the assembly any role in the formation of a new government. The convention prevailed, and the assembly voted itself out of existence. If the radicals lacked experience in colonial affairs, their strength lay in their organizational ability, their ability in 1775–1776 to recruit a large pool of volunteers, their intimate knowledge of the wharves, docks, and streets of Philadelphia, and their exhilaration at the taste of power.[9]

The key to resistance in South Carolina was the idea of harmony. The South Carolina elite valued the internal unity and stability of their society. Newly rich and self-confident, the aristocracy cultivated consensus and unity because they feared that their prosperity and freedom were precarious. South Carolina enjoyed the most buoyant economy of any American colony. British permission in 1730 to export rice directly to the Iberian peninsula, an exception to the mandatory shipment of staple crops to the mother country, made rice fabulously profitable trade and touched off soaring economic growth. Indigo, which could be raised on ground unsuitable for rice, was also a high-profit export. With its splendid harbor and proximity to the West Indies, Charles Town became a major port. In the 1740s the prosperous lowland planters and Charles Town merchants coalesced into a closely knit ruling class that dominated the Commons House of Assembly as the Virginia gentry did the House of Burgesses. Factionalism disappeared as the planter-merchant aristocracy found it had little to fight about and much to gain from control of the colony's government. This social harmony was imperative because, for all their wealth and success, the elite felt isolated and insecure. Huge slave importation made the economy productive; but slaves outnumbered whites by as many as seven to one in parts of the lowland, and whites lived in constant fear of black insurrection. The colony was militarily vulnerable to Indian attacks on its western frontier and to Spanish invasion from Florida until Britain acquired the region in 1763. Because of its growth and wealth, Charles Town was an ideal dumping ground for British office seekers—or placemen—who were dependent on the Crown for their livelihood and occupied most of the appointive positions on the council and customs service not already under control of the assembly. Native South Carolinians viewed them with contempt.

Because it condemned selfish factions and celebrated the integrity and patriotism of the individual, the Country ideology was enormously influential among the South Carolina elite. Those writings literally told South Carolinians that they were virtuous and capable. To protect themselves against Indians, slaves, or British officialdom, South Carolinians concluded that they must place the interests of the whole community above personal gain and that the highest applause should be accorded to men who followed the dictates of conscience. The pre-Revolutionary controversy greatly heightened the relevance of these ideas. British measures and administration seemed an external plot to break the power of the planter-merchant elite. Once violated by outsiders, the freedom, harmony, and stability of the colony might never be restored.

During the Stamp Act crisis mobs forced Lieutenant Governor William Bull to remove the stamps to a British warship for safety and compelled the stamp distributor to resign. To avoid using tax-bearing customs documents, the port of Charles Town was closed. With nearly 1,400 unemployed, restive sailors in the town, the merchants put enormous pressure on Bull, and in late January 1766 he allowed the port to reopen without the use of stamped clearance papers. In this irregular way violence and disorder were avoided until June, when news of the repeal of the Stamp Act finally arrived.

A major controversy over customs enforcement developed in 1767 when Daniel Moore, a new customs collector, arrived in the colony and began applying the tighter requirements of the Sugar Act to Charles Town commerce. These provisions made it much easier for customs agents to seize ships on suspicion of smuggling and then secure from the vice-admiralty judge a "just cause" ruling if evidence of wrongdoing did not materialize on the confiscated vessel. (Just cause rulings protected the agent from prosecution in civil courts for damages arising from false seizure and allowed for the sale of part of the confiscated cargo to pay the costs of the prosecution, including the customs agent's fee.) In the flourishing South Carolina economy there was little incentive to smuggle, but by long tradition merchants and customs officials had established an expeditious and loose system of customs searches. Moore was determined to break the power of the merchants by terminating practices that speeded the flow of goods at the cost of strict enforcement. He may have been trying to enrich himself from confiscated cargoes. He decided to make an example of the richest and most powerful Charles Town merchant, Henry Laurens. In 1768 five of Laurens's ships were seized on dubious technicalities. The vice-admiralty judge, Egerton Leigh, a placeman who had married Laurens's niece, tried to arrange a compromise. He dismissed all of the charges against Laurens but granted just cause rulings in all but one of the seizures. The last seizure was, in fact, an unsuccessful attempt to blackmail Laurens, who was offered return of the vessel by the customs agents in exchange for Laurens's dropping a civil

ℏℏℏℏℏℏℏℏℏℏℏℏℏℏℏℏℏℏℏℏℏℏℏℏℏℏℏℏℏ

A LIST of the Names of *those*

who AUDACIOUSLY continue to counteract the UNIT-
ED SENTIMENTS of the BODY of Merchants thro'out
NORTH-AMERICA; by importing British Goods
contrary to the Agreement.

John Bernard,
    (In King-Street, almoft oppofite Vernon's Head.

James McMafters,
        (On Treat's Wharf.

Patrick McMafters,
      (Oppofite the Sign of the Lamb.

John Mein,
    (Oppofite the White-Horfe, and in King-Street.

Nathaniel Rogers,
    (Oppofite Mr. Henderfon Inches Store lower End
    King-Street.

William Jackfon,
    At the Brazen Head, Cornhill, near the Town-Houfe.

Theophilus Lillie,
    (Near Mr. Pemberton's Meeting-Houfe, North-End.

John Taylor,
    (Nearly oppofite the Heart and Crown in Cornhill.

Ame & Elizabeth Cummings,
(Oppofite the Old Brick Meeting Houfe, all of Bofton.

Ifrael Williams, Efq; & Son,
    (Traders in the Town of Hatfield.

And, *Henry Barnes,*
    (Trader in the Town of Marlboro'.

---

*The following Names fhould have been inferted in
the Lift of Juftices.*

County of Middlefex.	County of Lincoln.
Samuel Hendley	
John Borland	John Kingfbury
Henry Barnes	
Richard Cary	County of Berkfhire.
County of Briftol.	Mark Hopkins
George Brightman	Elijah Dwight
County of Worcefter.	Ifrael Stoddard
Daniel Blifs	

ℏℏℏℏℏℏℏℏℏℏℏℏℏℏℏℏℏℏℏℏℏℏℏℏℏℏ

38 A 1770 blacklist of merchants who openly violated the nonimportation agreement.

suit in the one seizure not protected by just cause. The whole experience turned Laurens from a political maverick, who had even opposed resistance to the Stamp Act, into one of the most eloquent and passionate organizers of resistance in South Carolina.

Enforcement of nonimportation in 1769 combined the colony's desire to be just as patriotic as Boston with the need for internal unity. To enforce the boycott a committee of thirteen planters, thirteen merchants, and thirteen artisans was created. Rather than allow artisans to become a clamorous opposition, the elite had absorbed the leaders of this segment of society into the establishment, a step that greatly aided nonimportation enforcement. The committee clashed dramatically with a few obstreperous men who had the audacity to cite personal conscience as a ground for resisting regimentation by the community. But rather than jeopardize the fragile unity of support for resistance, the committee winked at most violations.

Irritated by charges that they merely supported steps taken first in Boston, the South Carolina Whigs took the initiative, and in 1769 the Commons House contributed £1,500 to the Wilkesite Society of the Supporters of the Bill of Rights. Outraged, Hillsborough ordered the governor of South Carolina to veto the assembly's appropriation bills unless they contained an express prohibition on any further expenditure of public funds outside of the colony without the concurrence of the royal council and governor. This royal instruction created a constitutional crisis because the Commons House had enjoyed since the 1730s exclusive control over expenditure, a power that was the cornerstone of self-government in South Carolina. The Commons House refused to pass the prohibition and thereafter was unable to appropriate any funds—although by 1774 it found ways of spending public monies by issuing to the colony's creditors certificates of payment, which then circulated as a kind of paper money. In the Wilkes Fund controversy, the Crown had insisted that the Commons House humble itself in a gesture of obeisance to British authority; nothing could have angered or radicalized South Carolina leaders more than this affront to their sense of honor.

All of these patterns of resistance—mobs confronting physically weak British forces and officials, informal networks of Sons of Liberty working within disaffected segments of society and communicating across colonial lines, town and provincial committees of correspondence speaking in behalf of the will of the people, assemblies forced to defend their legislative existence—began as attempts by the community to preserve existing liberties and then

95

suddenly became something more dynamic and unpredictable. These collective acts of resistance signified that the people were drawing themselves into a posture of uprightness, conscious in a new way of their virtue and maturity. The full extent of that assertion of political adulthood became clear when the Second Continental Congress voted to create an army and just over a year later declared independence. The willingness to prepare for war and to become a free people was a supreme test of political intellect and radical nerve. While this final step was taken by people in every colony, the leaders of the Virginia aristocracy did so with exceptional reluctance, thoughtfulness, and finally swiftness and grace.

Although they were deeply in debt to British creditors and living beyond their means, there is no reason to doubt the sincerity of the remarkable generation of aristocratic planters and members of the House of Burgesses who led Virginia to independence and statehood. Their political creed perfectly expressed their social needs and group interests. A public-spirited, conscientious aristocracy, they lived integrated, dutiful, rewarding lives tending to their plantations, handling export of their tobacco and a host of financial matters, supervising their slaves, marrying off their children advantageously, managing their local Anglican vestries, operating local government as justices of the peace, and serving in the House of Burgesses. It was a way of life demanding hard work, attention to detail, cultivation of friendship with kinsmen and contemporaries, and financial acumen. Once convinced that the Crown wanted to reduce them to a servile status, their resistance was immediate and vigorous.

The pre-Revolutionary controversy coincided with a crisis of confidence among the Virginia planters. Financially overextended, the planters had great difficulty earning enough sterling with their tobacco exports to remain solvent. After the death in 1766 of John Robinson, who had been Speaker of the Burgesses and Treasurer of the colony, it was discovered that he had embezzled vast amounts of public funds to help his friends cope with these financial difficulties. The scandal shook the confidence of the elite and reminded them at a crucial time of the frailty of human nature and the corrupting influence of power. Political deference by the mass of small farmers to the planter leadership remained strong, but religious dissent, especially among Baptists, expressed, in part, the loathing that common farmers felt for planter social preeminence. The planters knew, without admitting it, that the lynchpin of their social system was slavery. The vast importation of slaves during the years from 1670 to 1730 had transformed the labor system and made the colony rich from slave-produced exports; slavery also produced enough prosperity to lift the once-poor white population up to the level of respectable middle-class farmers and tradesmen. In this way slavery freed the colony of the menace of a poor, white, idle, and violent lower class of former indentured servants. In the place of that danger now came the ever-present possibility of slave insurrection. The masters tried to stabilize the labor system by promoting skilled, responsible slaves to a higher status and better level of care, but these acculturated slaves, with whom the masters could talk and relate, became the organizers of covert slave resistance. The splendid plantation society of Virginia aristocrats was riven with these stresses and tensions.

These growing strains made the planters extremely reluctant to force a breach with the mother country. When Patrick Henry in 1765 introduced five resolutions in the Burgesses attacking the Stamp Act, four moderate ones passed by narrow margins while a fifth calling Parliamentary taxation "illegal, unconstitutional, and unjust" was rejected as too extreme. As late as the spring of 1776, Landon Carter—who had denounced British policy over the preceding decade on moral and constitutional grounds and more vehemently than Henry—found the prospect of independence horrifying. The crisis of confidence among the Virginia gentry had another political consequence. Deeply imbued with Enlightenment ideas about the wholeness of human life and convinced that mankind had a noble destiny, Virginians constructed a moral view of their society. Abstract and idealized, this moral perception was a blueprint for holding together the diverse elements of the social order in time of crisis.

No documents expressed the moral vision of the Virginia

patriots so well as Jefferson's *Summary View of the Rights of British America* written in the summer of 1774 and the Declaration of Independence drafted two years later. Both expressed techniques of resistance because they put into words for the first time views that already commanded broad support and used language with unprecedented vividness and power. Both dealt with basic issues of strategy at the precise moment when decisions about tactics were being made. Both attributed the political energy of the people to their moral heritage.

Sickness kept Jefferson from attending the convention in Williamsburg that selected Virginia's delegates to the First Continental Congress. He intended that his *Summary View* should be used as the official instructions for the chosen delegates, but the convention rejected it in favor of a more legalistic defense of colonial rights. Published as a pamphlet, *Summary View* placed the then

39　Thomas Jefferson.

obscure Virginia planter in the first rank of American political theorists. A historical treatise, it sought to show that Parliament had no jurisdiction in America and that the colonists owed allegiance only to the king. The Saxon settlers of England were the prototypes of free people governed by their own institutions and uncontaminated by sophistication or excessive power. They were therefore vigorous and self-reliant. The Norman invasion of 1066 robbed the Saxons of their birthright, Jefferson asserted, but they never consented to this deprivation of their liberty. In the same way, the settlers of the colonies had brought with them natural rights to liberty and had never relinquished them. This discovery of the colonists' natural rights and of the vigor and strength to maintain them, Jefferson realized, changed the way Americans perceived the Empire. By refusing to feel subordinate, the colonists were in fact affirming that the colonies and the British Isles were equal, coordinate branches of the same Empire. That equality, that breathtaking sense of political adulthood, existed in the consciousness of people because it was right. "Let no act be passed by any one legislature" within the Empire "which may infringe on the rights and liberties of another. This is the important post in which fortune has placed you," Jefferson told his contemporaries, "holding the balance of a great, if well poised Empire."[10]

Within two years the whole attempt to renounce Parliament and preserve the colonies' place in the Empire collapsed. But the Declaration of Independence was infused with the same idea that universal moral truths liberated people by filling them with an overwhelming sense of their own ability and duty. Jefferson's technique for communicating this view was derived from Scottish rhetorician William Duncan's system of rhetoric, in which the key word was "self-evident." Jefferson's major and minor premises led not only to a logical conclusion but also to a realization that one's moral intuitions, alerted by the steps of the argument, were right. Major premise: "We hold these truths to be self-evident, that all men are created equal, that they are endowed by their creator with certain unalienable rights, that among these are life, liberty and the pursuit of happiness." Minor premise: "to secure these rights, govern-

ments are instituted among men, deriving their just powers from the consent of the governed." Conclusion: "whenever any form of government becomes destructive of these ends, it is the right of the people to alter or to abolish it. . . ." The whole document is filled with arguments following that format. Jefferson later said that the Declaration was only a statement of the "common sense of the subject" and "an expression of the American mind." By assigning the highest priority to natural rights, consent of the governed, and the right of revolution, Jefferson was placing these values above other American beliefs in maintaining the social order, providing people with security for their lives and property, maintaining public virtue, and even insuring the rule of law. His experience as a Virginian in a time of deep uncertainty required that those moral purposes of government take precedence over the conventional tasks of the state. Only in that way could he justify the awful step of instituting a "new government, laying its foundation on such principles and organizing its powers in such form, as . . . seem most likely to effect [the people's] safety and happiness."

Notes

[1] David S. Lovejoy, *Rhode Island Politics and the American Revolution, 1760–1776* (Providence: Brown University Press, 1958), p. 158.
[2] Nathan O. Hatch, "The Origins of Civil Millennialism in America: New England Clergymen, War with France, and the Revolution," *WMQ*, XXXI (1974), 407–30.
[3] Quoted in Edmund S. Morgan, "The Puritan Ethic and the American Revolution," *WMQ*, XXIV (1967), 10.
[4] Eli W. Caruthers, *A Sketch of the Life and Character of . . . David Caldwell* (Greensboro, 1842), pp. 273–84.
[5] Quoted in Bernard Bailyn, *The Ideological Origins of the American Revolution* (Cambridge: Harvard University Press, 1967), p. 94.
[6] *Ibid.*, p. 319.
[7] Richard D. Brown, *Revolutionary Politics in Massachusetts* (Cambridge: Harvard University Press, 1970), pp. 147–48 and ch. 4.
[8] Stephen Lucas, "Between Protest and Revolution: The Ideology of Reconciliation and the Popular Debate over Independence," in the *Proceedings* of the St. Augustine Conference on American Loyalism, to be published in 1977.
[9] R. A. Ryerson, "Political Mobilization and the American Revolution: The Resistance Movement in Philadelphia, 1765–1776," *WMQ*, XXXI (1974), 582–83.
[10] Quoted in Merrill Peterson, *Thomas Jefferson and the New Nation* (New York: Oxford University Press, 1970), p. 75.

40   Public reading of the Declaration of Independence.

Bibliography

The outstanding works on colonial resistance are Merrill Jensen, *The Founding of a Nation: A History of the American Revolution, 1763–1776* (New York: Oxford University Press, 1968), and Bernard Bailyn, *The Ideological Origins of the American Revolution* (Cambridge: Harvard University Press, 1967). In their approach to the Revolution, their handling of evidence, and their treatment of motivation, ideology, and the political process, the two books could hardly be more dissimilar. Yet they are alike in their mastery of enormously complex material. Bailyn's concern is with the "assumptions, ideas, and beliefs that lay behind the manifest events of the time"; Jensen's "emphasis is on the deeds of men rather than on their motives and their rhetoric."

Bailyn's *Ideological Origins* is a revision of his book-length introduction to *The Pamphlets of the American Revolution, 1750–1776*, vol. 1, *1750–1765* (Cambridge: Harvard University Press, 1965). His introductions to the various pamphlets are extremely valuable, and in particular his essay on John Dickinson on pp. 660–67 is a concise statement of his whole interpretation of Revolutionary radicalism. Bailyn's *Origins of American Politics* (New York: Alfred Knopf, 1968) carries the search for the beginnings of colonial resistance into the forgotten decades of the 1730s and 1740s. His *Ordeal of Thomas Hutchinson* (Cambridge: Harvard University Press, 1974) and his edition of Hutchinson's "Dialogue Between a European and an American Englishman" in the 1975 volume of *Perspectives in American History* reconstruct the experience of one of the most knowledgeable and tragic of the American loyalists.

Next in importance among broad-gauge studies of colonial resistance are Edmund S. and Helen M. Morgan, *The Stamp Act Crisis: Prologue to Revolution* (Chapel Hill: University of North Carolina Press, 1953); Bernard Knollenberg, *The Origin of the American Revolution, 1759–1766* (New York: Macmillan, 1960) and *The Growth of the American Revolution, 1767–1775* (New York: The Free Press, 1974); Jack P. Greene, *The Quest for Power: The Lower Houses of Assembly in the Southern Royal Colonies, 1689–1776* (Chapel Hill: University of North Carolina Press, 1963); Pauline Maier, *From Resistance to Revolution: Colonial Radicals and the Development of American Opposition to Britain, 1765–1776* New York: Alfred Knopf, 1972); and H. Trevor Colbourn, *The Lamp of Experience: Whig History and the Intellectual Origins of the American Revolution* (Chapel Hill: University of North Carolina Press, 1965).

A number of books deal with the impact of religion on Revolutionary society. Carl Bridenbaugh, *Mitre and Sceptre: Transatlantic Faiths, Ideas, Personalities, and Politics, 1689–1775* (New York: Oxford University Press, 1962) discusses the role of the Anglican Church in colonial politics.

102

Alan Heimert, *Religion and the American Mind From the Great Awakening to the Revolution* (Cambridge: Harvard University Press, 1966); Richard Bushman, *From Puritan to Yankee: Character and the Social Order in Connecticut, 1690–1765* (Cambridge: Harvard University Press, 1967); Rhys Isaac, "Religion and Authority: Problems of the Anglican Establishment in Virginia in the Era of the Great Awakening and the Parsons' Cause" and "Evangelical Revolt: The Nature of the Baptists' Challenge to the Traditional Order in Virginia, 1765–1775" *WMQ*, XXX (1973), 3–36, and XXXI (1974), 345–68; and Adrian C. Leiby, *The Hackensack Valley in the Revolutionary War* (New Brunswick, N. J.: Rutgers University Press, 1962) deal with interdenominational tensions between rationalists and evangelicals. Bernard Bailyn, "Religion and Revolution: Three Biographical Studies," *Perspectives in American History*, IV (1970), 85–169 cautions against any simple equation of evangelicalism with libertarianism, and William G. McLoughlin, "The Role of Religion in the Revolution: Liberty of Conscience and Cultural Cohesion in the New Nation," in Stephen G. Kurtz and James H. Hutson, eds., *Essays on the American Revolution* (Chapel Hill: University of North Carolina Press, 1973), argues that the founding fathers sought to use religion as a source of cultural cohesion for the new nation.

On specific controversies between Britain and the colonists, see David S. Lovejoy, "Rights Imply Equality: The Case Against Admiralty Jurisdiction in America, 1764–1776," *WMQ*, XVI (1959), 459–84; Benjamin Woods Labaree, *The Boston Tea Party* (New York: Oxford University Press, 1964); Hiller B. Zobel, *The Boston Massacre* (New York: W. W. Norton, 1970); Arthur M. Schlesinger, Sr., *The Colonial Merchants and the American Revolution, 1763–1776* (New York: Columbia University Press, 1918); David Ammerman, *In Common Cause: American Response to the Coercive Acts* (Charlottesville: University of Virginia Press, 1974); Jack P. Greene, "Bridge to Revolution: The Wilkes Fund Controversy in South Carolina, 1769–1775," *Journal of Southern History*, XXIX (1963), 19–52; Donald C. Lord and Robert M. Calhoon, "The Removal of the Massachusetts General Court from Boston, 1769–1772," *Journal of American History*, LV (1969), 735–55; and Alan Rogers, *Empire and Liberty: American Resistance to British Authority* (Berkeley and Los Angeles: University of California Press, 1974).

Among the most illuminating accounts of resistance that focus at the local and colonial levels are Jere Daniell, *Experiment in Republicanism: New Hampshire Politics and the American Revolution, 1741–1794* (Cambridge: Harvard University Press, 1970); Robert E. Brown, *Middle-Class Democracy and the Revolution in Massachusetts, 1691–1780* (Ithaca: Cornell University Press, 1954); Richard D. Brown, *Revolutionary Politics in Massachusetts: The Boston Committee of Correspondence and the*

Towns, 1772–1774 (Cambridge: Harvard University Press, 1970); Robert
Taylor, *Western Massachusetts in the Revolution* (Providence: Brown Un
versity Press, 1954); David S. Lovejoy, *Rhode Island Politics and th
American Revolution, 1760–1776* (Providence: Brown University Pres
1958); Oscar Zeichner, *Connecticut's Years of Controversy, 1750–17*.
(Chapel Hill: University of North Carolina Press, 1949); Roger Char
pagne's articles "Family Politics vs. Constitutional Principles: The Ne
York Assembly Elections of 1768 and 1769," *WMQ*, XX (1963), 57–7
"New York and the Intolerable Acts, 1774," *New York Historical Socie*.
Quarterly, XLV (1961), 195–207; "New York Politics and Independenc
1776," *New York Historical Society Quarterly*, XLVI (1962), 281–303; an
"New York's Radicals and the Coming of Independence," *Journal of Ame*
ican History, LI (1964), 21–40; Milton M. Klein, *The Politics of Diversit*
Essays in the History of Colonial New York (Port Washington, N. Y.: Ke
nikat Press, 1974); Larry Gerlach, *Revolution or Independence: Ne*
Jersey, 1760–1776 (New Brunswick, N. J.: Rutgers University Press, 1976
David Jacobson, *John Dickinson and the Revolution in Pennsylvani*.
1764–1775 (Berkeley and Los Angeles: University of California Pres
1965); David Hawke, *In the Midst of a Revolution* (Philadelphia: Unive
sity of Pennsylvania Press, 1962); David Curtis Skaggs, *The Roots of Mar*
land Democracy, 1753–1776 (Westport, Conn.: Greenwood Press, 1973
Ronald Hoffman, *A Spirit of Dissension: Economics, Politics, and the Rev*
olution in Maryland (Baltimore: Johns Hopkins University Press, 1974
Charles S. Sydnor, *Gentlemen Freeholders: Political Practices in Washing
ton's Virginia* (Chapel Hill: University of North Carolina Press, 1952
Richard Beeman, *Patrick Henry: A Biography* (New York: McGraw-Hil
1974); Hugh Lefler and William S. Powell, *Colonial North Carolina: A
History* (New York: Scribner's, 1973); Robert M. Weir, "'The Harmony W
Were Famous for': An Interpretation of Pre-Revolutionary South Carolin
Politics," *WMQ*, XXVII (1969), 474–501 and *"A Most Important Epocha"*
The Coming of the Revolution in South Carolina (Columbia: University o
South Carolina Press, 1970); W. W. Abbot, *The Royal Governors o
Georgia, 1754–1775* (Chapel Hill: University of North Carolina Press
1959); and Kenneth Coleman, *The American Revolution in Georgi*
(Athens: University of Georgia Press, 1958).

On Thomas Jefferson and the Declaration of Independence, see in partic
ular Wilbur S. Howell, "The Declaration of Independence and Eighteent
Century Logic," *WMQ*, XVIII (1961), 463–84, Merrill Peterson
Thomas Jefferson and the New Nation (New York: Oxford University
Press, 1970), pp. 37–96, and Cecelia M. Kenyon, "The Declaration of Inde
pendence," in *Fundamental Testaments of the American Revolution*
(Washington, D.C.: The Library of Congress, 1973), pp. 25–46.

There is an important body of recent work on "the American Revolution

Seen From the Bottom Up," including an essay with that title by Jesse Lemish in Barton Bernstein, ed., *Towards a New Past: Dissenting Essays in American History* (New York: Pantheon, 1968), and also Lemish's "Jack Tar in the Streets: Merchant Seamen in the Politics of Revolutionary America," *WMQ*, XXV (1968), 371–407 and "Listening to the 'Inarticulate': William Widger's Dream and the Loyalties of American Revolutionary Seamen in British Prisons," *Journal of Social History*, III (1969), 1–29. R. A. Ryerson, "Political Mobilization and the American Revolution: The Resistance Movement in Philadelphia, 1765–1776," *WMQ*, XXXI (1974), 565–88 reconstructs the membership, social composition, and motivation of pre-Revolutionary committees in Philadelphia.

For contrasting views on the nature of Revolutionary radicalism see Hiller B. Zobel, "Law Under Pressure: Boston, 1769–1771," in George A. Billias, ed., *Law and Authority in Colonial America: Selected Essays* (Barre, Mass.: Barre Publishers, 1965), Pauline Maier, "Revolutionary Violence and the Relevance of History," *Journal of Interdisciplinary History*, II (1971), 119–35, Jesse Lemish, "Radical Plot in Boston (1770): A Study in the Use of Evidence," *Harvard Law Review*, LXXXIV (1970), 485–504, James H. Hutson, "An Investigation of the Inarticulate: Philadelphia's White Oaks," *WMQ*, XXVIII (1971), 3–26 and, Jesse Lemish and John K. Alexander, "The White Oaks, Jack Tar, and the Concept of the Inarticulate," *WMQ*, XXIX (1972), 99–134.

Finally, there is a category of scholarship that seeks to identify broad social, psychological, and cultural imperatives compelling Americans to declare their independence in 1776. Edwin G. Burroughs and Michael Wallace, "The American Revolution: The Ideology and Psychology of National Liberation," *Perspectives in American History*, VI (1972), 167–306, and Winthrop D. Jordan, "Familial Politics: Thomas Paine and the Killing of the King, 1776," *Journal of American History*, LX (1973), 294–308, deal with the psychology of independence. James Kirby Martin, *Men in Rebellion: Higher Government Leaders and the Coming of the Revolution* (New Brunswick, N. J.: Rutgers University Press, 1973), and John M. Head, *A Time to Rend: An Essay on the Decision for American Independence* (Madison: State Historical Society of Wisconsin, 1968) present alternative interpretations of social and political frustration.

On slavery and revolution in Virginia, see Gerald W. Mullin, *Flight and Rebellion* (New York: Oxford University Press, 1972) and Edmund S. Morgan, *American Slavery, American Freedom* (New York: W. W. Norton, 1975).

War 3

If the war is restored to the central position that it had for the Revolutionary generation, and if it is seen not only as an instrument but as a process which entangled large numbers of people for a long period of time in experiences of remarkable intensity, then it may be possible to bring the study of the war and the study of the Revolution more closely together.*

John Shy

BRITISH CONDUCT OF THE WAR

Traditional scholarship on the War for Independence has concentrated on how the patriots won the conflict—Washington's skills as strategist and commander, the contribution of the French alliance, and the sacrifices and courage of the Continental Army. Over the past two decades a great deal of additional work has been done on the causes of British defeat, not only the immediate background to the British surrender at Yorktown but the whole range of mis-

* John Shy, "The American Revolution: The Military Conflict Considered as a Revolutionary War," in Stephen G. Kurtz and James H. Hutson, eds., *Essays on the American Revolution* (Chapel Hill: University of North Carolina Press, 1973), p. 124.

judgments and miscalculations that undercut the effectiveness (
British arms in Revolutionary America. Historians are now ju.
beginning yet another kind of inquiry, which in place of the olde
preoccupations with victory and defeat conceives of the war as
social process, explores the impact of the struggle on communit
life, and probes the attitudes of Americans toward mobilizatior
social and economic dislocation, political instability, and violenc
all of which accompanied the military struggle.

Like the Vietnam war in its effect on the United States, the W;
for Independence enmeshed Britain in a limited war, across a
ocean, in a wilderness setting where she lacked the manpower an
logistics to occupy every disaffected locality or destroy the enemy
main force. Like the South Vietnamese, Britain's supporters i
America, the loyalists, were militarily and politically inferior t
the insurgents. Like the American commitment, Britain's decisio
to impose a military solution originated with bureaucrats—expert
in the mechanics of imperial administration—who had a narro*
view of the nature of colonial society. Certain that the colonist
were quarrelsome, unruly children, British officials who dealt wit
colonial policies could not comprehend the depth and extent of th
movement for independence. As the war dragged on and succes
eluded British arms, the ministry resorted consciously and uncor
sciously to misrepresentation of Britain's standing in the conflic
in order to persuade a suspicious Parliament to continue to financ
the venture. Finally a collapse of public confidence forced Britai
to negotiate a withdrawal. While the parallel between the two wai
is not exact, the structural similarities between the American Rev
olution and the Vietnam war emphasize the ways in which bot
wars were complex social phenomena with roots deep in the pol
tics, culture, and psychology of the participating societies.

Britain's decision in the summer of 1775 to use military me;
sures to subdue colonial resistance, as well as the implementatio:
of that decision during the following twelve months, were both th
products of a complex political situation. Nothing illustrates bette
the mixture of personality, factional politics, and bureaucracy tha
shaped British policy than the principal events in London relatin

THE AMERICAN STATES DURING THE WAR FOR INDEPENDENCE

NEW HAMPSHIRE

Fort Stanwix
Saratoga
Bennington
Connecticut River
BOSTON
Oriskany
NEW YORK
Hudson River
MASSACHUSETTS
RHODE ISLAND
CONNECTICUT

Delaware River
PENNSYLVANIA
NEW YORK

Germantown
PHILADELPHIA
NEW JERSEY
Brandywine
MARYLAND
DELAWARE

Potomac River
Chesapeake Bay

Yorktown
James River
ATLANTIC
OCEAN

VIRGINIA

NORTH CAROLINA

Guilford Courthouse

Moore's Creek

Kings Mountain
Cape Fear
WILMINGTON

Cowpens
Camden
Ninety-Six
SOUTH CAROLINA
CHARLESTON

GEORGIA
SAVANNAH

- cities and towns
○ locations of battles and other events
— proclamation line of 1763

WEST FLORIDA
(British)

ST. AUGUSTINE

PENSACOLA

EAST FLORIDA
(British)

0   100   200   300
Miles

to the colonies, and their consequences in America, from the autumn of 1774 until the end of 1776:

In late September 1774 Lord North's ministry received reports from General Gage in Boston that imposition of the Coercive Acts was proceeding without serious difficulty. Then after a seven-week silence, Gage wrote—in a letter received on November 18, 1774—that all New England was in a state of rebellion and that the whole region would have to be occupied by British troops before order could be restored. The ministry was furious with Gage—more for sending unexpectedly bad news than for failing to appreciate the gravity of the situation earlier.

By Christmas the resolutions of the First Continental Congress—including its nonimportation-nonexportation boycott—had reached London. Convinced that Gage's inactivity and caution were to blame for the spreading contagion, the ministry on January 27, 1775, ordered him to use force against the leaders of the rebellion in Massachusetts.

In February Parliament resolved that Massachusetts was in a state of rebellion and passed a Restraining Act prohibiting New England from trading with the rest of the Empire.

Gage's orders to use force reached him on April 14, 1775, and five days later he sent 700 British regulars to seize rebel powder at Concord. A skirmish with colonial militia assembled on Lexington Green, Lexington, serious fighting at Concord, and a humiliating retreat under fire back to Boston turned an incipient rebellion into a full-scale war.

Gage's intended replacement, General William Howe, arrived in Boston in late May, though he would not assume command of the British army until September. On June 17 the British suffered heavy casualties in the course of driving the rebels from Breed's Hill overlooking Boston.

On August 14 the Olive Branch petition from the Second Continental Congress arrived in London while Colonial Secretary Dartmouth was at home in Staffordshire. George III reacted angrily by issuing on August 23 an order in council for immediate measures to quell the colonial rebellion.

On October 22 the ministry ordered an expedition to the southern colonies. These troops were to rendezvous with back-country North Carolina loyalists, who were expected to march to Wilmington.

On November 10 Dartmouth—a pious and gentle man who had little stomach for coercive measures—stepped down as Colonial Secretary and was replaced by Lord George Germain, a vigorous organizer and firm advocate of harsh colonial measures.

41 A contemporary and accurate sketch by Amos Doolittle of British troops firing on colonial militia on Lexington Green, April 19, 1775.

Anxious to offset Germain's powerful position within the ministry and fearful of the strain that a prolonged war would place on the stability of his government, Lord North, in December 1775 and January 1776, arranged for a peace commission that would make one last effort to resolve the imperial controversy before Britain unleashed the full power of her arms. North proposed that General Howe's brother, Admiral Richard Howe, go to America as commander of the fleet and peace negotiator.

Ever since the spring of 1775 British officials had realized that Boston should be abandoned and New York City made the hub of British military operations, but General Howe was not able to evacuate Boston until March 1776. He took his troops to Halifax, Nova Scotia. Then in June and July Howe moved 9,000 troops to Staten Island, where they were joined by Admiral Howe's fleet, 6,000 more British troops from other parts of the Empire, and 5,000 Hessian mercenaries (hired soldiers from Germany).

111

42 A British view of the Revolutionary militia, "The Yankie Doodles Intrenchments Near Boston 1776."

As peace commissioner, Admiral Howe first held an abortive conference with a delegation from Congress. On August 23–25 General Howe drove Washington's green and outnumbered army on Long Island from the field of battle into an indefensible position in Brooklyn. Howe did not follow up this victory quickly or ruthlessly enough to destroy the rebel force. Washington and his troops were able to escape to Manhattan.

After Admiral Howe made another fruitless attempt to negotiate with Congress, General Howe devoted September and October to the task of occupying New York City, but he did it in such a leisurely fashion that Washington was able to retreat safely to a defensive line near White Plains, New York.

When Howe decided not to attack the Continental Army, Washington was able to move his troops to safety across the Hudson into New Jersey and then to Pennsylvania.

General Howe spent the remainder of 1776 occupying northern New Jersey, and although the rebel regime there virtually collapsed, looting by Hessian and British troops so alienated the populace that Howe was unable to consolidate his initial gains.

In counterattacks at Trenton on December 26, 1776, and at Princeton on January 2, 1777, Washington demonstrated that his ragged army could still fight and bolstered the sinking morale of the Revolutionary movement.

At work in these events was a variety of personal and political forces. First, the king, the Solicitor General, and the Attorney General formed the core of an influential group that from mid-1774 onward wanted to use military measures to restore Parliamentary authority in America. Ranged against them were Lord North, Colonial Secretary Dartmouth, and a scattering of officials in the bureaucracy and members of Parliament—including the Howe brothers—who were apprehensive about the collision course on which Britain and the colonies were embarked. North found that maintaining a Parliamentary majority required endless attention to detail, and he had little appetite for the added burden of managing a war. Dartmouth, a captive Rockingham Whig, had little political clout within the ministry, and his influence had steadily declined: by late 1774 he did little more than relay the ministry's instructions to colonial governors. Accelerating the decline in North's and Dartmouth's influence over colonial affairs was the sudden ascendency of Germain, who badly wanted Dartmouth's job and steadily gained new supporters within the ministry and Parliament in 1775.

Once safely installed as Colonial Secretary, Germain sabotaged Lord North's final effort at conciliation by getting Admiral Howe's negotiating powers trimmed to the point that he had no meaningful concessions to make to the colonists. Only if a colony would cease all participation in the activities of the Continental Congress could Howe suspend the act restraining its trade with the rest of the Empire. As a result of these maneuvers, direction of the war oscillated between two conflicting requirements—the Howes' desire to secure colonial submission at the lowest cost in terms of lives, money, and political inconvenience and Germain's determination to vindicate Parliamentary authority over the colonies once and for all. Both were rational objectives and they were not entirely incompatible. But the existence of two different conceptions of the military situation inhibited Britain from maximum vigor and single-mindedness to the struggle.

Both of these conceptions of the war shaped British conduct throughout 1777. General Howe believed that the steady advance of his army through the middle colonies would force Washington into demoralizing retreat and attract a growing stream of colonists back to adherence to the Crown. Howe knew that only a minority of the colonists were committed loyalists, but he expected that the bulk of the population would acquiesce in support of whichever side could gain predominant military advantage in the most heavily populated regions. The war itself, however, unleashed powerful disruptive forces that undermined the validity of Howe's diagnosis. Looting by British and Hessians in New Jersey during the autumn and winter of 1776 crippled pacification there. The loyalists who took up arms in support of the British in the middle colonies were too often bent on revenge and the settling of private vendettas. They were as much a liability as an asset to the British.

In his desire to avoid large-scale battles, General Howe allowed weeks and then months of valuable time to be lost. He first re-

43   British troops under General William Howe occupy New York City in September 1776.

jected an overland march to Philadelphia in the spring of 1777 as too risky. Then he took months to prepare a naval expedition. En route to Philadelphia he decided against sailing up the Delaware River and chose the Chesapeake Bay instead. After an overland march through Delaware and Pennsylvania, he entered Philadelphia on September 26, 1777, months behind schedule. Germain had ordered General John Burgoyne in Quebec to march south into New York and down the Hudson Valley; he expected Howe to occupy Philadelphia in time to move northward and link up with Burgoyne somewhere in the lower Hudson Valley late in the summer of 1777. The plan miscarried for two reasons. First Burgoyne misjudged how difficult it would be to move an army through the wilderness between the St. Lawrence and Hudson valleys. His army of British regulars, loyalists, Indians, French-Canadian civilians, and women campfollowers was not the sort of tough, indomitable force to overcome all the obstacles they encountered. Then in August 1777 Burgoyne lost nearly 800 men when he sent Hessian Colonel Frederick Baum on a raid into southern Vermont. New Hampshire militia ambushed and destroyed Baum's force at the Battle of Bennington. Hopelessly surrounded and cut off by General Horatio Gates, Burgoyne surrendered at Saratoga, New York, on October 18, 1777. The second reason Germain's plan failed was that he had never made it clear to Howe that he was to move with dispatch against Philadelphia so that he would have time to march north in support of Burgoyne during the summer of 1777. Germain distrusted Howe, knew that he had powerful allies in Parliament, and he was unable to send Howe more troops without alarming Parliament about the cost of the war. Germain therefore felt that he could not put pressure on Howe to act more aggressively. The Colonial Secretary's political weakness in dealing with the commander of British forces in North America undercut the strategic boldness of his plan to have Howe and Burgoyne sever New England from the other rebellious colonies.

The British defeat at Saratoga did more than scuttle Britain's timetable for ending the war; it exposed serious—and previously

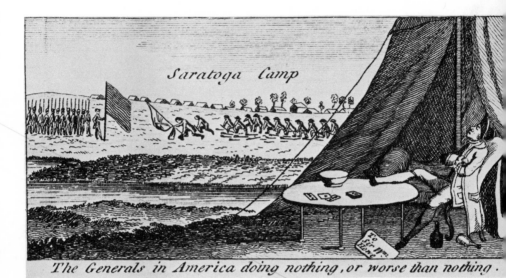

Saratoga Camp

The Generals in America doing nothing, or worse than nothing.

44 A British caricature of General William Howe dozing in comfort in Philadelphia while Burgoyne surrenders at Saratoga.

hidden—flaws in the ministry's will to govern and in its ability to use power realistically and competently. Indeed, the gradual deterioration of intelligent, purposeful administration in London from 1778 to 1781 is an instructive lesson in the nature of power politics. British officials continued throughout these years to function rationally; at the same time, British ministers and generals seemed to lose touch with reality. They became preoccupied with the damage the war was doing to their individual reputations, and they tended to interpret every piece of good news as evidence that the war was nearly won and to discount the mounting evidence of patriot resiliency and tenacity. This failure of perception and judgment did not occur because the ministry was unusually stupid. Rather, it occurred because the ministers lacked the public support and military talent needed to bring the war to a successful conclusion, and in preference to facing that reality, they first deceived themselves and then the rest of Parliament about the seriousness of the situation.

News of Saratoga, which reached London in December 1777, and French entry into the war the following February triggered major changes in Britain's posture in the war. Changes occurred in command, in grand strategy, in the role of sea power, and in the political problems facing the ministry. Lord North knew the war was lost and tried to resign, but the king and the ministry—fearing political chaos—prevailed on North to remain head of the government. As soon as he learned of Burgoyne's defeat, General Howe asked to be relieved of command. Most of the ministry were afraid of the dislocations that would accompany a change in commander in chief and wanted Howe to stay at his post. Germain thought otherwise and prevailed on his colleagues to accept Howe's resignation. Howe's subordinate, General Henry Clinton, was named to the post. Clinton was a thoroughly professional soldier and a more aggressive field commander than Howe, and he understood better than any other high British official the relationship of sea power to land operations. With France in the war, Clinton realized, Britain would need to maintain naval superiority in waters off New York City and adjacent to any region in the southern states where British troops might be operating during the remainder of the war. In addition, Britain would need to keep enough ships in the Caribbean and the English Channel to protect the British West Indies and homeland itself from French attack. Finally, British ships would have to continue to furnish British garrisons in America with virtually all of their supplies. Clinton knew how to calculate the effects of the shifting naval balance upon the land war, but the fleet commanders who succeeded Admiral Howe in 1778 did not share Clinton's sense of naval strategy. Moreover, the ministry in London and especially the First Lord of the Admiralty did not realize that Britain did not have enough ships to perform all of those vital tasks. Public fear of French attacks against the English coast forced the ministry to keep close to home ships desperately needed in American waters.

The need to stem criticism of the conduct of the war—and the simultaneous need to develop a new strategy for winning it—sapped the ministry's capacity to govern. A series of acrimonious disputes erupted in late 1778 and early 1779, first between two British admirals over which of them should be blamed for a partial French naval victory in June 1778, and then between Germain and General Howe over Howe's conduct of the war. During a subsequent Parliamentary inquiry into Howe's conduct, Howe argued that the rebellion in America enjoyed wide popular support and that he had done everything possible to crush it militarily, while Germain contended that the majority of the population was loyal to the Crown and that Howe had let victory slip through his fingers. The result of these controversies was to spread distrust and suspicion throughout the government and the military. Henceforth, Germain would be afraid to offend Clinton—lest his new commander in chief resign in protest—and Clinton would spend much of his time making certain that subordinates and superiors took responsibility for any decision that might turn out badly.

The heart of Britain's response to Saratoga was a revamped grand strategy that combined a realistic scaling down of military objectives with deceptive estimates of the cost of attaining those goals. First, Britain abandoned hope of a clearcut victory in the northern states by evacuating Philadelphia and preserving a large reservoir of manpower in New York City. Drawing upon these forces if necessary, Britain then planned to subdue the southern states, starting with Georgia, then South Carolina and North Carolina, and finally Virginia. North also sent a new peace commission to America empowered to grant every colonial demand short of complete independence. The whole plan assumed that the numerous loyalists in the southern back country would augment regular British forces and enable Britain to pacify the southern states as soon as British regulars defeated American forces in the region. Dependence on loyalist support, of course, made the strategy extremely risky. The ministry made no serious effort to determine whether southern back-country loyalists could be relied upon to flock in large numbers to the king's standard once British regulars invaded the region. Nor did the ministry even comprehend the difficulties of pacifying a conquered state and reconciling a defeated populace.

The mirage of loyalist support in the South became the central ingredient in the ministry's plans. Loyalist exiles in London had testified for the government against General William Howe, effectively discrediting Howe's claim that Britain could not win the war. Now the ministry felt obligated to listen closely to loyalist military advice. The new reliance on southern loyalist support, furthermore, helped answer the embarrassing question of why the war was lasting so long. The resource of loyalist support had always been there, the ministry explained plausibly, and now the loyalists would enable Britain to gain quick control in 1780–1781 of a large region from Georgia to Virginia; by implication this position of strength would enable Britain to negotiate an honorable withdrawal from the war. Besides, the ministry told the scrupulous "country-independent" members of Parliament, Britain had a moral obligation to help the loyalists recover their place in colonial society.

Britain's new strategy began auspiciously in late 1778. The peace commission that visited America in the summer of 1778, to be sure, failed completely to interest Congress in a negotiated peace. But the commissioners did recommend to the ministry that civil government be restored as soon as possible in New York City and in Georgia as soon as that state was captured. In late December 1778 and early January 1779 British and loyalist troops from New York City and St. Augustine, East Florida, swept lowland Georgia free of patriot forces in a stunning coordinated attack and occupied both Savannah and Augusta. Throughout 1778 and 1779 Clinton skillfully deployed British naval forces in the Caribbean and Atlantic to prevent the French navy from cutting British supply lines. In October 1779 the British repulsed a French attack on Savannah, and as soon as the French fleet departed, Clinton led an 8,000-man force from New York to South Carolina. He landed south of Charles Town in February 1780, cut off escape routes from the city, and on May 11, 1780, forced the American commander, General Benjamin Lincoln, to surrender the city. Within a few weeks the British were in control of the entire state. Clinton returned to New York City, leaving the command of the southern campaign in the hands of General Charles Cornwallis. In August Cornwallis won a stunning conventional battlefield victory at Camden, South Carolina, over the Continental troops who had been rushed south following the fall of Charles Town.

45   The interior of an eighteenth-century French warship.

With the conquest of South Carolina and lowland Georgia and the victory at Camden, Britain finally seemed within reach of suppressing revolt in the southern and middle states. Cornwallis needed only to subdue the weak and disspirited American forces in North Carolina and then march north into Virginia for a link-up with British troops from New York. Yet fourteen months later he surrendered his army at Yorktown, Virginia, and British strategy was in ruins. Why? In large part, French sea power finally caught up with an overextended British navy. More fundamentally, the war created social turbulence that, while weakening the new state and Continental governments, played far greater havoc with British efforts to reimpose royal authority in America.

THE WAR AS A REVOLUTIONIZING PROCESS IN AMERICAN SOCIETY

In November 1778 a group of prominent loyalist refugees in New York City sought out a sympathetic British officer, Major Patrick Ferguson, and presented him with their appraisal of the war. The rebel cause, they insisted, was on the verge of collapse. The Continental currency was nearly worthless; taxes, conscriptions, and in-

ternal security operations had destroyed much of the popularity of state governments; the people's patience and will to endure further difficulties were nearly exhausted. One vigorous British campaign in the middle and Chesapeake states, the loyalists claimed, would place intolerable strains on the rebel regime and bring British victory.[1] Such loyalist advice—tendered a year after the American victory at Saratoga and six months after French entry into the war—was myopic and self-serving. But that should not obscure crucial elements of truth in what the loyalists were saying. The war had indeed caused serious dislocations in American society, and these shocks had confronted Revolutionary governments with the need to reorganize American political institutions into more responsive, adaptable, and functional bodies.

The depreciation in the value of Continental currency—which struck the loyalists as an intolerable evil that would soon destroy patriot morale—was the prime example of a social stress that helped create a new political order in Revolutionary America. In June 1775 Congress created a currency by issuing $2,000,000 in notes that were not legal tender but were intended as a temporary medium of exchange with which the Congress could support its new

121

army. The army was vastly more expensive than anyone had anticipated. Profiteering in supplies was scandalous, and few purchasing officers had experience in money management. As costs soared, Congress printed more money and its value depreciated. When Congress finally called a halt in 1779 after issuing $200,000,000, the value of this money had dropped to one-thirtieth of its 1775 value. Congress simply passed to the states responsibility for supplying the army.

The states could not bear that burden, and by 1780–1781 both states and Congress resorted to seizing supplies and forcing hapless suppliers to accept worthless "loan certificates." Foreign loans also took up some of the slack. The social consequences of this currency system were pervasive. Depreciation of the money supply had the effect of spreading the cost of supporting the war as widely throughout society as money actually circulated. Acceptance and use of Continental and state currency and loan certificates greatly expanded the number of people involved in the support of the war. And the profits that sharp merchants were able to obtain in a sellers' market created a new breed of rich Americans hungry for social recognition and political power.[2]

46   General Henry Knox's headquarters, guarded by one of his famous cannons.

The creation of armed forces to fight the war further politicized American society by thrusting the Revolution into the lives of individuals and forcing them to make concrete choices about their conduct. The patriots used two kinds of military organization: the state militia and the Continental Army. Each affected the course of the Revolution differently, and each reflected particular sources of revolutionary energy.

The Revolutionary militia was simply a revival and perpetuation of the colonial militia, which had deteriorated since the 1750s but remained a familiar public institution. Raised locally for short periods of service, poorly trained and equipped, undisciplined and prone to flee under fire, the Revolutionary militia has long had a bad historical reputation. The important fact about the militia, however, was not its fighting ability but rather its very existence. Militia service was an effective screening mechanism for identifying differing degrees of Revolutionary allegiance. Those who refused militia duty created the suspicion that they were loyalists. If a man shirked duty or was a troublemaker, he invited investigation and interrogation. For the mass of militiamen who were merely reluctant, the routine of drill and periodic mobilization involved them—sometimes against their preferences—in active support of the Revolution. In several states militiamen elected their own officers and resisted regimentation at the hands of aristocratic patriot leaders; while such conduct weakened the efficiency of patriot regimes, this distrust of authority was consistent with the ideology of the Revolution. In this way militia service broadened the sense of participation in a revolt against arbitrary authority.

The very weakness of the militia was also its strength. If citizen soldiers went home to plant or harvest crops or because they just got tired of fighting, they also reassembled just as quickly and spontaneously. The militia provided an enormous pool of manpower to augment the Continental Army. The militia were not much help in heavy fighting, but their sheer numbers—often more than half of the American troops in any battle—shielded Continental regulars and prevented the annihilation of whole units of the regular army. The militia did not need an elaborate supply system. 123

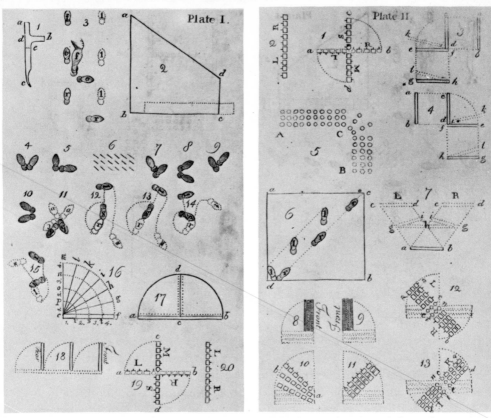

47 Drawings from Timothy Pickering, *An Easy Plan of Discipline for a Militia*, showing (in Plate I) an all-purpose tool, patterns for making cartridges, and marching drill diagrams; and (in Plate II) diagrams for marching by column of ranks.

In the last resort, when all resistance collapsed in South Carolina in the summer of 1780, unofficial, irregular militia companies formed and instigated savage guerilla warfare. "It is not the number of troops Mr. Washington can spare from his army that is to be apprehended," wrote a British officer; "it is the multitude of militia and men in arms ready to turn out at an hour's notice at the show of a single regiment of Continental troops" that frustrated British offensive operations.[3]

If the militia was an instrument of Revolutionary coercion at the local level, the Continental Army was the visible manifestation of a national Revolutionary government. Supplied and administered by Congress, the army consisted of a middle department com-

124

manded by General Washington and embracing operations from southern New York to Maryland, as well as smaller southern and northern departments subject only to loose supervision by Washington. Congress controlled the appointment of generals; the states appointed junior-level officers. Each state raised and organized its own unit, which was called the "line" of that state—the Virginia line, the Rhode Island line, etc. For most of the war Washington had between 6,000 and 12,000 regular troops in the middle department, while 2,000 to 3,000 served in both the northern and southern departments.

Like any new bureaucracy, the army and its civilian administrators were inefficient, decentralized, and quarrelsome. During the 1777–1778 winter encampment at Valley Forge, food supplies dwindled to three ounces of meat and three pounds of bread per man per week, and shoeless soldiers wrapped their bleeding feet in rags. That same winter a disgruntled clique of officers and Congressmen undermined Washington's authority with a campaign of whispered criticism, to which the commander in chief overreacted in a rare display of petulance. The army was a flawed institution because it had to accommodate itself to conflicting demands of its own soldiers and officers and of Congressional and state officials as well. There was, for example, a high incidence of desertion and reenlistment by soldiers anxious to collect multiple enlistment bounties. Corrupt contractors made huge profits selling shoddy and overpriced goods to the army. Unpatriotic and financially ruinous as those practices were, such greed and corruption was the price paid to enlarge the proportion of the population actively involved in the Revolutionary struggle. The army was an institution that could convert human flaws into military strength.

Although its victories at Saratoga and Yorktown were crucial to the winning of the war, the army's most important characteristic was its ability to function over long periods of time in a position of inferiority to the British and from that weakened posture to sap the strength and vitality of the enemy. Simply by raising 8,000 new troops in the spring of 1777 and securing French supplies, Congress enabled Washington to thwart Howe's first plans for an overland

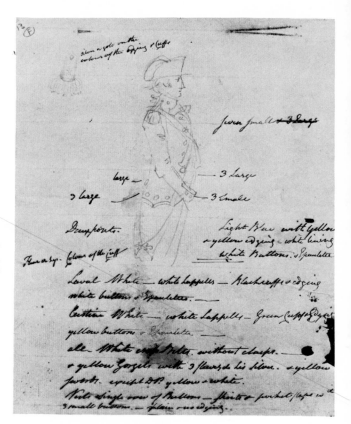

48 A page from the sketchbook of artist John Trumbull, colonel in the Continental Army, showing an infantryman with notes on colors and trappings.

march to Philadelphia. When Howe finally entered the city in September 1777, he sensed that his expedition into Pennsylvania was a failure. The populace—reputedly filled with neutralists and loyalists—was sullen and withdrawn. In two clashes with the Continental Army—at Brandywine Creek on September 10 on the march to Philadelphia and at Germantown on October 3 as the British occupied the region just north of the city—Howe drove the Americans from the field of battle, but they retreated in good order and remained intact. The limits of British power were clear: the steady conquest of populous territory did not cause the army nor the Congress to disintegrate. Then, from the autumn of 1778 until late summer 1781, Washington's army encamped in a long crescent around the British stronghold at New York City, one extending

126

from Danbury, Connecticut, through the Hudson highlands and reaching Elizabeth, New Jersey. The British could not regain the initiative, in part, because Washington's force kept 3,000 to 4,000 extra combat troops tied down in idleness in the New York garrison.

Nathanael Greene, a Rhode Islander and former Quaker nominated by Washington to take command of the southern army following the Battle of Camden, proved the most adroit American general in turning military inferiority to his own advantage. With only 1,600 ragged, ill-equipped regulars at his disposal in December 1780, Greene boldly divided his army, assigning the best troops to Colonel Daniel Morgan. Using two lines of militia as a shield, Morgan lured the British Legion, the crack loyalist cavalry unit under the command of Lieutenant Colonel Banastre Tarleton, into a superbly executed tactical trap at the Battle of Cowpens on January 17, 1781. Each line of militia fired one volley and then retreated to the side of the battlefield. Slowed and disorganized by the militia volleys but believing that the Americans were in retreat, the British charged forward. The Continental regulars surprised them with a counterattack, and the militia rejoined the en-

49 The legendary "Molly Pitcher," who, according to tradition, carried water to her husband at the Battle of Monmouth and, when he was killed, took his place loading cannons.

counter from the side of the battle. The panic-stricken British and loyalist troops were caught in a trap, from which only Tarleton and a few of his men escaped. Robbed of his mounted strike force, Cornwallis felt compelled to crush Greene's army. From January 30 to February 14, 1781, Cornwallis chased Greene across North Carolina. Winter rains made fording the numerous rivers and streams in the region extremely hazardous. Greene had arranged for boats to carry his men across the Dan River into southern Virginia. There he could resupply and secure fresh recruits in safety. Lacking any means of crossing the Dan and exhausted from the chase, Cornwallis abandoned the pursuit. As an aftermath to British triumphs in South Carolina, this "race to the Dan" put Continental and British troops on a more even footing. It exhausted Cornwallis's seasoned regulars, forced him to jettison much of his equipment, and extended his line of supply 150 miles across the state of North Carolina. It turned what was to have been a triumphant procession in strength across North Carolina into a desperate, disorderly pursuit.

50a An unknown Continental soldier sketched by John Trumbull.

50b General Horatio Gates sketched by John Trumbull.

Visible, disciplined, and patient, the Continental Army learned through adversity how to operate effectively from a position of inferiority. By the end of the war its officers believed that they had saved the republic from destruction. They saw the militia as undisciplined, untrained bumpkins, whose shortcomings repeatedly jeopardized the American cause. Spontaneous, pervasive, and popular, the militia was, in fact, a key part of the local infrastructure of the Revolution. Leaders at the state level valued the militia because it seemed to them an admirably republican form of military organization. It posed no threat to civilian institutions, had no haughty officer class, and was thoroughly decentralized.

The struggle for American independence also acted to dislocate and politicize the black population. The war undermined and jeopardized the institution of slavery and offered free and enslaved black Americans unprecedented opportunities to improve their lot. Between 40,000 and 50,000 slaves—a tenth of the slave population of the states—won their freedom as a direct or indirect result of the War for Independence. Half of that number sought the protection of the British army, served the Crown in a military or civilian

129

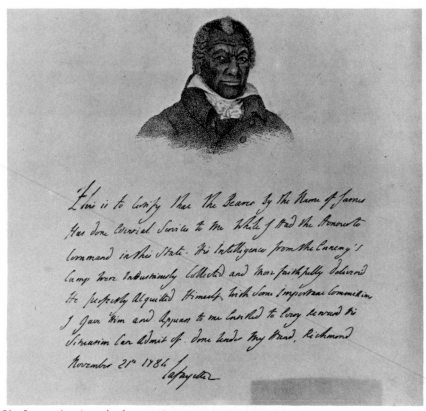

51 James Armistead, slave and spy in the Virginia campaign, with General Lafayette's handwritten commendation. Armistead was freed by the Virginia general assembly in 1786 for service "at the peril of his life."

capacity, and were evacuated with British soldiers and white loyalists when the British departed from North America in 1782–1783. The other 20,000 to 25,000 lived in Pennsylvania or in New England, where gradual or complete emancipation occurred by the end of 1784. (New York and New Jersey did not abolish slavery until the nineteenth century.) A smaller number, perhaps 5,000 to 10,000, won their freedom by serving in the Continental Army, state militia, or aboard American naval vessels or privateers. In many cases masters sent their slaves to serve as substitutes when they were drafted into military service or enlisted their slaves in order to qualify for land grants, cash bonuses, or

130

duty pay given to each recruit. In every state, free blacks provided a pool of labor from which hard-pressed patriot officials obtained military and civilian manpower. Runaway slaves, posing as free blacks, volunteered for war-related jobs or enlisted in the armed forces as a way of covering their escape from their masters.

The war not only provided slaves with opportunities to escape bondage or to earn their freedom; it also fostered the movement to abolish slavery altogether. Quakers and blacks themselves organized successful abolition campaigns in Pennsylvania, Massachusetts, Rhode Island, and Connecticut. In South Carolina Henry Laurens and his son, Colonel John Laurens, became converted to the cause of the abolition of slavery. John Laurens led a personal crusade to emancipate slaves who would enlist and serve in the Continental Army. Congress approved the plan, which provided financial compensation to the owners of slaves who took up arms in the American cause. But South Carolina and Georgia planters, outraged at the idea of placing guns in the hands of slaves, killed Laurens's plan. "Prejudice, avarice, and pusillanimity," Laurens declared, had thwarted this revolutionary experiment in warfare and human relations.[4] The leaders of the Virginia aristocracy—who

52   A sketch by John Trumbull of a Connecticut officer and his black servant at the Battle of Breed's Hill.

53 Deborah Sampson Gannett, a black woman who disguised herself as a man, enlisted in the 4th Massachusetts Regiment, and was decorated for her "extraordinary . . . heroism."

were among the most ideologically fervent patriots—took the lead of freeing some of the slaves who had contributed their labor to the American cause. In 1782 Virginia dramatically simplified its manumission statute, which set forth procedures by which a master could legally free his slaves. Probably intended as a first step toward abolition of slavery in Virginia, the new manumission law was shortlived. By the late 1790s fear of slave insurrection in Virginia inspired a stream of new legislative restrictions on manumission.

In spite of the limited advances in the status of blacks between 1775 and 1784, the war did not fundamentally reduce racial exploitation in America. The British could not champion the cause of the slaves without alienating the numerous slave-owning loyal-

54 British troops evacuating Charles Town take captured slaves with them to the West Indies.

ists in South Carolina and Georgia. In November 1775 Governor Dunmore of Virginia issued a proclamation offering freedom to slaves of patriot planters who would leave their masters and fight for the restoration of royal authority. He excluded from his offer the slaves of his own loyal supporters among the aristocracy. Although 800 blacks joined Dunmore and were enlisted in Dunmore's Ethiopian Regiment, the proclamation actually galvanized the Revolutionary movement in Virginia by outraging and alarming the planters. In South Carolina in the summer of 1775, a black ship pilot named Jeremiah Thomas allegedly told other blacks that they should join the British in putting down the colonial rebellion. The Whigs hanged and burned him as an example to other restive blacks. Slaves apparently realized that the Revolutionary Whig regimes, especially in Virginia and South Carolina, were strong enough to inflict swift and terrible vengeance on slaves who would attempt their own rebellion in 1775 and 1776.

The most serious threat to the cohesion of American society during the war occurred in regions where substantial numbers of people either openly sympathized with the British or withheld their support from the new Revolutionary government. Some of these people did not believe that they could transfer their allegiance from the king to the United States; others were desperate or unprincipled people to whom the Revolution presented irresistible opportunities to improve their lot in life at the expense of Whig neighbors; still others were politically inexperienced or bewildered people who understood little of the dispute with Britain. Many shared some combination of these attitudes. Taken together, these disaffected people constituted a potential threat to the very survival of the Revolution. Because they were widely scattered and unorganized, however, that danger never fully materialized. But the apprehension they aroused among the patriots and their blatant refusal to imbibe the prevailing ideology of liberation and constitutionalism dramatized the political limitations of the Revolutionary governments and compelled patriot leaders to exercise their power prudently and deftly.

Vermont and the southern back country in North and South Carolina and Georgia provided one kind of setting for such patriot-loyalist conflict. These regions lacked the established institutions, dominant political families, and settled traditions that characterized the mature political communities on the seaboard where resistance usually flourished. These frontier areas had experienced rapid

55 Loyalist refugees en route to new homes in northern Canada camping on the banks of the St. Lawrence River.

settlement during the pre-Revolutionary generation. With development came the emergence of local elites of ambitious, hard-driving, well-connected men, who were often volatile and touchy about their honor and their interests. Being on the losing side in the Revolution could destroy all they had gained, while being on the winning side would vastly increase their wealth and influence; hence their loyalties vacillated according to which side they perceived as most likely to achieve final victory.

Until set up as an independent state in 1777 (although not admitted into the Union until 1791), Vermont had been called the New Hampshire Grants, a region disputed between colonial New York and New Hampshire. Since the early 1760s there had been a rising influx of New England settlers holding land grants from New Hampshire, and New York settlers, wealthy land speculators or their clients holding New York titles. In the excitement of 1775, two remarkable New England brothers, Ira and Ethan Allen used the collapse of British authority as an opportunity to seize control of the machinery of county government set up by New York in the 1760s and expel New Yorker speculators. Sporadic mobs then ter-

rorized some well-to-do New Englanders who had close ties with New York interests. These men were forced to acknowledge the legitimacy of the Revolution or to declare themselves loyalists, flee to Quebec, and take up arms for the Crown. By the time Burgoyne arrived in the region in July 1777, with some of these Vermont loyalists in tow, allegiances in the state were extremely fluid. Hundreds of men volunteered to help build a road for Burgoyne's cumbersome army to follow. It was this show of support that led Burgoyne to assume that he was in friendly territory and to send forces under Colonel Baum into southern Vermont to seize rebel arms, resulting in the British defeat at the Battle of Bennington and the loss of nearly 800 of Burgoyne's men. The government of Vermont retaliated swiftly by confiscating the property of the most prominent loyalists who had fought with the British or collaborated openly with Burgoyne, but it was done in such a way that the fragile social order of the young region was tampered with as little as possible. Most of the land confiscated was quickly sold to patriot relatives of accused loyalists. To maintain the state's independence, Ira and Ethan Allen needed a broad base of support. When New York blocked Vermont's bid for recognition by the Continental Congress, the Allens undertook secret negotiations with the British—seeking British recognition of the state's independence and access to the commerce of Quebec in return for Vermont's withdrawal from the war. Although these negotiations never reached any agreement, the Allens did maintain a discreet alliance with a large number of covert loyalists in the state. A spasm of violence in 1775–1776 had created an independent Vermont, but the Allens had succeeded because they refused to perpetuate the kind of corrosive, internecine conflict that would only frighten people anxious to maintain legal title to their land.

Similarly, the southern back country was a fluid society of newcomers with a weak system of political institutions; these factors led to patriot-loyalist conflicts in 1775–1776. In North Carolina a widely scattered and diverse population of Highland Scots, Scots-Irish, German-speaking and English settlers had never coalesced into a unified political community. Opposition to British policy was strong but limited to pockets in the coastal lowlands, the Neuse and Roanoke river valleys in the east, and the two western counties of Rowan and Mecklenberg. The great influx of recent settlement lay in a broad, politically neutral belt in the upper Cape Fear River valley and central Piedmont region. With the aid of a Scottish officer in the British army and a handful of his own agents, Governor Josiah Martin succeeded in encouraging back-country supporters—chiefly newly arrived Scottish settlers on whom he had lavished generous land grants—to prepare to fight against the rebels. Though forced to take refuge on a British war-ship, Martin received word on January 3, 1776, that a British expe-dition had been dispatched to the mouth of the Cape Fear River, the site of the town of Wilmington; and he called on the back-country loyalists to rise, march to the coast, and occupy Wil-mington in advance of the arrival of British regulars. By February 14, 1776, 1,400 volunteers—two-thirds of them Highland Scots—assembled in the upper Cape Fear. At first successful in eluding a force of rebel militia, the loyalists headed south for Wil-mington, but other patriot troops positioned themselves on wooded slopes on the bank of a creek in the path of the loyalists' line of march. Rashly trying to cross a partially dismantled bridge, which crossed Moore's Creek, the loyalists were completely routed by cannon fire. When General Clinton, commanding the British ex-pedition to the Carolinas, learned of the disaster, he canceled his plans to land troops at the mouth of the Cape Fear.

In the South Carolina back country the loyalists had far better leadership than in North Carolina, and with almost no help from the royal governor they came very close to seizing control of the South Carolina–Georgia frontier in the summer and fall of 1775. The Whig leadership dominated the lowland aristocracy and the Charles Town merchant community; and in the first six months of 1775 the Whigs seized effective control of the lowlands, forcing the newly arrived governor, William Campbell, to seek refuge on a British warship in Charles Town harbor. The device that the South Carolina Whigs employed was an "Association," or oath, which all inhabitants were required to sign. When they tried to secure signatures in the back country, however, the new council of safety encountered stubborn resistance. The most powerful figure in the region, militia Colonel Thomas Fletchall, an enormously overweight and vain figure, was irked at not receiving a more important position in the Revolutionary movement, and he successfully blocked efforts to require all militiamen in the back country to sign the Association. Playing on Fletchall's vanity and influence, a number of committed loyalist leaders sensed an opportunity to make their region a bastion of British strength at the very moment imperial authority was rapidly eroding everywhere else. Not a single militiaman under Fletchall's command signed the Association; instead they adopted a counter-Association denying that the king had forfeited their allegiance or violated the British constitution.

At this critical juncture, the Sons of Liberty in the Georgia back country seized and tortured Thomas Brown, an obstinate landowner recently arrived from Great Britain, by jabbing burning splinters into the soles of his feet. The enraged Brown escaped, made his way to District Ninety-Six in the western portion of South Carolina, and became a fiery leader of the growing loyalist movement there. The council of safety sent one of its most politically adroit members, William Henry Drayton, to District Ninety-Six to counter the influence of the loyalist leadership. By skillful maneuver, Drayton managed to separate Fletchall from the loyalist leaders and negotiate in September 1775 a truce between Fletchall's militia and the Whig forces. The truce collapsed in late November, and more than 2,000 rallied to arms to fight for the Crown against a patriot force of 550. A blizzard occurred, which made marches and discipline extremely difficult, and after three days the fighting sputtered out and the loyalists dispersed. The loyalists had been waging a defensive campaign, most of them just wanting to be left alone. The Whigs had a more clearly defined aim: to discredit the leadership of the ambivalent Fletchall and the intransigent loyalists. The lack of a cohesive community and the hazards of life in the back country gave the Whigs a decisive advantage.

Another characteristic location for patriot-loyalist conflict was in settled regions in which social unity and political leadership were fractured by a variety of suspicions and jealousies, class and religious antagonisms, and rival conceptions of the nature of the good society. Such settings for internal conflict occurred in the Mohawk and Hudson river valleys in New York, in parts of southeastern Pennsylvania and Delaware, and on the eastern shore of Maryland. For many reasons, groups of people in these regions perceived in the Revolution a threat to the stability of their society and felt driven by desperation or anger to throw the weight of their support on the side of the British.

The Mohawk Valley was the sharpest example of people divided over questions of social policy. The man responsible for that division was Sir William Johnson—a fabulous character who was born in Ireland in 1715, emigrated to America in 1737, and settled in the Mohawk Valley to manage the property of his uncle, who had married into the De Lancey family. As an Indian trader, land speculator, agent for the British government, and militia officer, he became deeply involved in the life of the Mohawk Indians, one of the tribes of the Iroquois nation. He learned their language and was inducted into their tribe; he built a huge home in the forest, where he resided with successive Mohawk mistresses, and sometimes he lived with the Indians and led them in battle wearing war paint and Indian garb. Johnson received vast gifts of Indian land and used all his influence to prevent the encroachment of white speculators into Indian territory. From 1754 until his death in 1774 he served as the Crown's Superintendent of Indian Affairs for the Northern tribes, and in 1768 he persuaded the British government to guarantee, in the Treaty of Fort Stanwix, Indian possession of land west of the old Proclamation line of 1763 in return for cession of a vast area east of that line. To Indians and white settlers alike, Johnson was an indulgent, baronial overlord, who expected only loyalty in return for gifts, loans, and protection. When he died, his son-in-law and nephew, Guy Johnson, succeeded him as Indian superintendent and used his vast influence with the Mohawks to insure that Indian warriors would help suppress the new colonial rebellion.

The use of Indians as counterrevolutionaries was, however, fraught with difficulty. They made up about a third of an offensive

139

By the Honorable Sir William Johnson Bar.t His Majesty's sole Agent and Super Intendant of Indian Affairs for the Northern Department of North America. Colonel of the Six United Nations their Allies and Dependants &c. &c.

To

Whereas I have received repeated proofs of your Attachment to his Britanic Majesty's Interests, and Zeal for his Service upon Sundry occasions, more particularly

I do therefore give you this public Testimonial thereof as a Proof of his Majesty's Esteem & Approbation. Declaring you the said   to be a   of Your
                      and recommending it to all his Majesty's Subjects and faithfull Indian Allies to Treat and Consider you upon all occasions agreable to your Character. Station, and Services.

Given under my Hand and Seal at Arms at Johnson hall the   day of   17

By Command of Sir W: Johnson

56   Indian certificate form used by Sir William Johnson.

strike force commanded by Lieutenant Colonel Barry St. Leger, which marched from Oswego on Lake Ontario in late July 1777 to rendezvous with Burgoyne near Albany, New York. Sir John Johnson, son of Sir William, led a group of Indians and white loyalists as a part of the St. Leger offensive, which ambushed and destroyed a patriot force at the Battle of Oriskany and in the aftermath burned a neutral village of Oneida Indians, another Iroquois tribe. That act destroyed the delicate web of Iroquois unity and provoked vengeful attacks by patriots and Oneidas upon Mohawk settlements. This mutual destruction of villages and crops in turn wiped out the food supply of Indians on both sides of the conflict; these tribes had so widely adopted the white man's agricultural techniques to the neglect of hunting that from 1777 onward famine and hunger became weapons of war that took a terrible toll. Deep divisions developed among white loyalists about the proper use of Indian warriors. Guy and John Johnson and their allies—Joseph Brant, a brilliant Mohawk leader, and his sister Mary Brant, Sir William's last Indian mistress—wanted the Indians to operate as a disciplined, elite, and independent military force. But Governor Guy Carleton in Quebec wanted the Indians to serve a defensive and subordinate role, and he placed them under the command of the Johnsons' rival, Colonel John Butler, a wealthy western New York loyalist. Butler preferred to recruit braves by getting them drunk, and therefore most of the Indians he recruited for the St. Leger offensive were so hungry and ill-clad that they did little fighting; when St. Leger's forces failed to capture Fort Stanwix and dispersed, the Indians robbed and assaulted retreating British and

57   Joseph Brant, Mohawk leader and British partisan warrior.

loyalist soldiers. With the surrender of Burgoyne at Saratoga, frontier New York ceased to be a strategic theater of the war, but it was nevertheless the scene of successive Mohawk and white loyalist terrorist attacks on patriot settlements and equally savage retaliation by patriots against Mohawk villages and crops.

Ever since the 1750s the British government had used its power to harmonize the interests of Indians and whites, and as a result of Sir William Johnson's ability and good fortune, large segments of the Iroquois nation, recently arrived white settlers, and wealthy landowners with commercial and political ties to the Crown comprised a coalition of support for Britain during the war. The fragility of Iroquois unity, the devastating impact of the war on the Indian economy, the mutual brutality of the fighting, and divisions among loyalist leaders weakened the capacity of these pro-British people to subdue the rebellion.

In contrast with the complex story of white-Indian relations in the Mohawk Valley, internal conflict in the Hudson Valley sprang from class conflict between landlords and tenants. In no other part of colonial America had agricultural tenancy been so predominant as on the great estates of the Hudson. The great landlords connected by marriage or political interest to the Livingston family generally became patriots, and their most deeply aggrieved tenants therefore tended to become loyalists; while the segment of the aristocracy led by the De Lancey family supported the Crown, and their tenants aligned themselves with the Revolution. The Livingston tenants had actually rioted against their landlords in 1766—inspired by the Stamp Act disorders in which the Livingstons had played a discreet role. In 1775 the tenants had the audacity to petition the New York Provincial Congress for relief from what they regarded as unfair leases, and by the autumn of 1776 nearly 400 Livingston tenants were armed and prepared to fight for the Crown. News of Burgoyne's offensive, however, touched off precipitate military preparations among these disaffected tenants, and the militia, which was firmly under the Livingstons' control, successfully rounded them up after a few brief skirmishes. Thereafter, tension between landlords and tenants in the Hudson Valley was strong. When the estates of loyalist landlords were confiscated and sold by the state of New York following the Revolution, many former tenants succeeded in purchasing on credit the land on which they lived—though within a few years most of these people were unable to make the annual payments and had to sell their farms to land speculators. On the estates of leading patriots, tenantry continued until the 1840s, and tenants remained an exploited, resentful social group.

Still another pattern of internal social conflict occurred on the eastern shore of Maryland. There the Revolutionary movement was in the hands of an alliance of powerful and wealthy families, led by Charles Carroll and Samuel Chase, which had only become politically organized as opponents of the proprietary government during the early 1770s. Determined to preserve the existing hierarchal social order, these Whig leaders lacked the broad appeal and widespread organization to rally the entire populace in support of the Revolution. Much of the population on the eastern shore were farmers and storekeepers, who resented the dominance of the Carroll-Chase regime and sought a greater dispersal of political power and economic opportunity. The predominance of such people on the eastern shore—and in isolated places on the western shore as well—nearly paralyzed the Revolutionary government. The militia on the eastern shore simply refused to obey officers appointed by the state government. Mobs stole valuable stores of salt from the homes of unpopular supporters of the Carroll-Chase administration, and popular feeling against the state's Revolutionary leaders nearly brought the enforcement of law to a halt. Thirty-four percent of those convicted of loyalist activity on the eastern shore were landless, and popular opinion compelled judges and juries to deal leniently with these people.[5]

A final prime location for patriot-loyalist conflict was in regions adjacent to British garrison towns. The British occupied Boston until March 1776; New York City from September 1776 until November 1783; Newport, Rhode Island, from December 1776 until October 1779; Philadelphia, from September 1777 until June 1778; Savannah, Georgia, from December 1778 until July 1782; Charles Town, South Carolina, from May 1780 until December 1782; Wilmington, North Carolina, from January 1781 until November 1781. 143

To these should be added two important garrison towns in the Floridas: Pensacola, which the Spanish captured in 1781, and St. Augustine, which Britain surrendered to Spain in 1784 under the terms of the Peace of Paris.

The garrison towns served as havens for loyalist refugees and as supply and naval bases and military headquarters for British forces. The British never restored civil government in any occupied part of America during the war—with the sole exception of coastal Georgia following the capture of Savannah from 1779 to 1782. Nevertheless, the British army did establish boards of police made up largely of loyalists in occupied New York, Philadelphia, and Charles Town and delegated to these bodies a wide variety of local government functions. This device gave loyalist civilians useful work to do and established the appearance of a successful pacification program. The most able and energetic of these loyalist administrators was Joseph Galloway in Philadelphia during the winter of 1777–1778. He assumed the duties of a powerful administrative overlord and initiated an amazingly comprehensive program of food and supply acquisition, military construction, intelligence gathering, internal security, price control, and poor relief. His wide contacts with loyalists throughout southeastern Pennsylvania—dating from his years of political experience as Benjamin Franklin's political lieutenant and speaker of the Pennsylvania assembly—and his intimate knowledge of the social and political divisions within Pennsylvania society served him well. But Britain's decision to abandon Philadelphia in the aftermath of Saratoga terminated Galloway's intelligent and promising efforts at pacifying an entire region to British rule.

The most important social consequence of garrison towns was the pressure they exerted on adjacent regions of patriot-held territory. The British presence in New York City and the immense buying power of the British army's commissary department created a vast amount of illegal smuggling of food stuffs from Fairfield County, Connecticut, and Bergen County, New Jersey. Both counties became sieves through which supplies, military deserters, British sympathizers, and criminals feeding on the chaotic situation passed between the British garrison towns and the patriot-held

58 British troops drilling on the Boston Common in 1768.

countryside. Violence in this twilight zone begot more violence. When a loyalist refugee in January 1778 in New York City returned to his home in Bergen County to visit a sick family, he was arrested and mysteriously shot in a scuffle with patriot militiamen. Loyalist agents from New York kidnapped two militiamen and turned them over to General Henry Clinton for execution. Disgusted with such amateurish heroics and fearful that British prisoners in American hands would be hanged in retaliation, Clinton refused to execute the pair of captives and finally ordered them exchanged. In 1780 Clinton reluctantly consented to the creation of a Board of Associated Loyalists, under the direction of former Governor William Franklin of New Jersey and other prominent loyalist exiles in New York City. The Associated Loyalists undertook a grandiose program of terrorist raids in Long Island Sound, New York State, and as far south as Frederick, Maryland. These actions did nothing to weaken patriot control of these areas, and they seriously embarrassed Clinton by infringing on his prerogatives as commander of British forces. Similarly, the loyalist exiles in St. Augustine, East Florida, were a violent and rootless

59   Newgate prison in Connecticut, a converted mine used to house loyalist prisoners.

band. Organized by the fiery Georgia loyalist, Thomas Brown, they turned the Georgia–East Florida border into a bloody irregular battlefield in 1776–1778, a situation that spurred the Whig regime in Georgia to redouble efforts at keeping the Revolution alive during the early years of the war.

THE PRICE OF VICTORY

In retrospect, the surrender of General Cornwallis at Yorktown, Virginia, in October 1781 appears a fitting and logical outcome to a long struggle in which British mistakes and American persistence combined to make American victory inevitable. There was, however, nothing certain about the outcome of Yorktown; the battle was the product of a cluster of circumstances that for a short period of time made Cornwallis vulnerable and rewarded Washington's patience and luck.

When Clinton completed the capture of Charles Town and the pacification of most of South Carolina in early June 1780 and prepared to return to New York City, he left Cornwallis in command of the British army in the South and issued him apparently general and flexible instructions. Cornwallis was to complete the pacification of South Carolina and Georgia—which seemed nearly accomplished—and next conduct an expedition into North Carolina, where he would rally the loyalists and render that state reasonably secure. Then Cornwallis was to march north into Virginia, where he would converge with British forces from New York and conduct a major offensive in the Chesapeake Bay area. Clinton, however, had a penchant for drafting orders and dispatches that would rebound to his credit if his plans succeeded but that would tie responsibility firmly to subordinates or superiors if anything went wrong. At the heart of his seemingly straightforward orders to Cornwallis was vagueness about the degree of success necessary in each state to justify the next stage in the movement toward the Chesapeake and about where Clinton's overall command of British forces in America superseded Cornwallis's direction of the southern offensive. It was no oversight that Clinton left those points obscure.

60 A sketch of Continental artillery engraved on the side of a powder horn.

The strategic weaknesses of the southern campaign became apparent as soon as Cornwallis tried to invade North Carolina in the early autumn of 1780. Clinton had saddled Cornwallis with two ungovernable subordinates, Major Patrick Ferguson and Lieutenant Colonel Banastre Tarleton, both commanding loyalist troops and both brilliant, reckless officers. Ferguson allowed himself to be cut off from Cornwallis's army by a huge force of "over the mountain men" from what later became Tennessee and trapped atop a spiney hogback ridge called Kings Mountain. In savage hand-to-hand combat on October 7, 1780, the patriot frontiersmen annihilated the loyalists. Tarleton's defeat at Cowpens in January 1781 further eroded the offensive power of British arms. Most North Carolina loyalists abandoned any idea of rallying to the king's standard, and a few who did try to rendezvous with Cornwallis—when he occupied the state capital at Hillsborough—fell into an ambush set by Colonel Henry "Lighthorse Harry" Lee. Bereft of loyalist support and bogged down in a hostile wilderness, Cornwallis lost a quarter of his men to death and injury in an inconclusive battle at Guilford Courthouse in March 1781. He marched to the port of Wilmington to be resupplied and then decided to risk an invasion of the Chesapeake rather than fight on in North Carolina or return to Charles Town and adopt a defensive position in South Carolina. He was now convinced that the war could be won only if Britain transferred all of its available forces to the Chesapeake. Germain had come to the same conclusion and was tactfully pressing Clinton to invade Virginia in force. In May 1781 Cornwallis marched into Virginia and joined a British force commanded by the American turncoat, Benedict Arnold. The

148

combined British force of 7,000 men ravaged parts of Virginia and in July retired to fortify Yorktown. Clinton remained skeptical of the value of this foothold in the Chesapeake. He considered the region a treacherous place to try to destroy American military strength, resented Cornwallis's good relations with Germain, and considered Cornwallis's march into Virginia as bordering on insubordination.

At this point the French admiral the Comte de Grasse made a bold decision to divert ships from the defense of the French West Indies in order to force a conclusion to the war on the North American mainland. This strategy required a coordinated French-American operation of extraordinary scope and intricacy. Admiral de Grasse sailed from Santa Domingo with 27 ships of the line—that is, carrying at least 74 guns and occupying a place in the line of battle—and 3,000 French soldiers; and Admiral Barras proceeded to Newport, Rhode Island, with messages informing the Comte de Rochambeau and Washington that de Grasse's destination was the Chesapeake. (Rochambeau and 5,500 French troops had been in Rhode Island since May 1780; Washington's headquarters were in Connecticut.) The French initiative forced Washington to abandon plans for an attack on New York City and to undertake what he regarded as a riskier and more difficult campaign in Virginia. This time everything fell into place. Washington ordered the Marquis de Lafayette, who commanded a small defensive force in Virginia, to try to keep Cornwallis from leaving Yorktown. Within a week of learning of de Grasse's destination, Washington and Rochambeau readied 7,000 Continental and French troops for the march to Virginia. Suspecting that this force would attack New York City, Clinton did not try to block their march southward. Meanwhile Barras slipped through a British blockade and brought Rochambeau's heavy artillery from Newport to the Chesapeake. Admiral de Grasse reached the bay on schedule and repulsed an attack by the British fleet under Admiral Samuel Graves. The British admiral did not know that Washington was marching to the Chesapeake, and he sailed to New York to resupply and refit his ships. When Barras arrived from Rhode Island, the French had thirty-six ships of the line and overwhelming naval superiority.

61 The Marquis de La-
fayette, who preceded
Washington to Virginia in
1781 to oppose Corn-
wallis's invasion.

By the time the seige of Yorktown began in early October, Washington had 5,700 Continentals, 3,200 militia, and 7,800 French soldiers against 8,000 British regulars, Germans, and loyalists. The
French artillery as well as that of the Americans under General
Henry Knox devastated the hastily constructed British fortifica-
tions. His position hopeless, Cornwallis surrendered on October
19, 1781. The loss of Cornwallis's army did not necessarily mean
that Britain had lost the war. Britain still held New York City,
Charles Town, and Savannah. But the defeat at Yorktown
destroyed the credibility of the ministry's military policy in
America. Lord North finally resigned, and Parliament voted to
cease hostilities in North America. A new ministry, led by Lord
Rockingham, proceeded to make peace.

The diplomacy of the American Revolution involved more than
sly old Ben Franklin cajoling France to intervene on the patriots'

behalf or the actual negotiation of the Peace of Paris. In addition to the French alliance and the peace treaty, the diplomacy of the Revolution encompassed the creation by American leaders of new concepts about international affairs, the intrigue of European diplomacy during the War for Independence, and the efforts by successive American envoys to create an effective style of personal diplomacy.

The colonial experience had enabled educated Americans to learn a great deal about European foreign policy without having to think about its application to the New World. Mercantilism taught them that the promotion of trade was the most important function of foreign policy and that European powers coveted the prospect of trade with North America. From the political infighting in Britain at the time of the Seven Years' War, the colonists learned of a deep division within British society between those who wanted Britain to maintain a balance of power in Europe through a close alliance with Prussia and diplomatic support for Hanover (the home of the royal family) and those who wanted Britain to stand aloof from continental power politics. From the writings of English radicals they learned that an adventurous, conniving foreign policy was characteristic of a corrupt, tyrannical ministry. Thomas Paine's *Common Sense* skillfully filled in the huge gaps in this conception of European diplomacy. European powers, he argued, would not support the American cause until independence was declared; the American states, he insisted, possessed ample timber to construct a navy strong enough to offset British sea power; France and Spain would be safe, dependable allies because their paramount interest in North America was access to American ports and markets.

These heady speculations about international power politics did not prepare the new republic for the practical difficulties of conducting foreign policy. In 1776 Congress sent three commissioners to France: Benjamin Franklin, Silas Deane, and Arthur Lee. Lee and Deane soon became implacable enemies because Deane used his position as American purchasing agent to rip off large personal profits in payoffs from French suppliers and in other ways intermingled government business with private transactions of his own. 151

Congress then split into two factions, one supporting Deane and another backing Lee, and for three years the conduct of foreign policy suffered. Franklin ignored the feud and skillfully lobbied for French aid. French entry into the war in early 1778 was the result of Franklin's personal diplomacy and the news of the British defeat at Saratoga. Spain and the Dutch Republic followed suit. In 1779 Congress replaced Deane and Lee with two new envoys of unimpeachable stature, John Jay and John Adams. Franklin remained ambassador to France; Jay went to Madrid and Adams to Amsterdam. As the result of French influence on Congress, the new diplomatic team was instructed to coordinate its activities closely with those of the French government. The American representatives found

62 The British Army marches in surrender out of Yorktown, Virginia, surrounded by French and American troops and the French fleet.

themselves caught in a complex cross fire of national interests. Spain did not want to recognize American sovereignty over territory west of the Appalachians, and the French postponed endorsing American independence as a peace provision until the Spanish got their way. Jay, who joined Franklin in Paris in June 1782, correctly diagnosed French tactics and proposed to Franklin that they thereafter act independently of France. Did Jay mean to violate Congress's instructions?—Franklin wanted to know. "*If* the instructions conflict with America's honor and dignity I would break them like this," Jay retorted, snapping the stem of his long clay pipe.

Serious tripartite negotiations between the British, French, and Americans then ensued and focused on five issues. Two major

American requirements for peace were recognition of American independence and the establishment of United States boundaries extending to the Mississippi River. Britain was willing to concede these demands but only after securing satisfactory compromise on three complex and difficult matters: British debts, loyalist property, and fishing rights off the coast of Newfoundland and Nova Scotia. At this point John Adams took the lead in the negotiations, and the compromises he struck reveal something of the political sophistication engendered in the Americans by the long military and political struggle. On the loyalist issue, Adams adamantly refused any restitution of property or compensation. The British explained that securing some satisfaction for their loyal adherents in America was a matter of national honor. "National honor, bosh," Adams replied. The loyalists had betrayed their own compatriots and had deceived Britain; they had no legal or moral claim on American compensation. The British abandoned their defense of the loyalists' interests, and the American negotiators agreed that Congress would "earnestly recommend" that the states restore the property of loyalists who had not gone into exile or borne arms in the war. Having forced the British to sacrifice the loyalists' interests, the Americans then freely conceded that British creditors could recover prewar debts in American courts. The fishing rights dispute boiled down to whether or not American fishing boats could go ashore on uninhabited coasts of Newfoundland and Nova Scotia to dry and cure their catch. Adams had talked with ship captains and merchants involved in North Atlantic fishing, and he was therefore able to propose mutually acceptable limitations on drying and curing. Fish, Tories, and debts finally put to rest, the treaty was signed.

Washington was an unseen participant in the effort to secure satisfactory peace terms. He realized that the Yorktown victory did not destroy British military power in America. Cornwallis's army represented only a quarter of British troops in North America. The French fleet in the Chesapeake would soon depart for the West Indies. The outcome at Yorktown did bring down the North ministry and destroy British public support for the war so that politi-

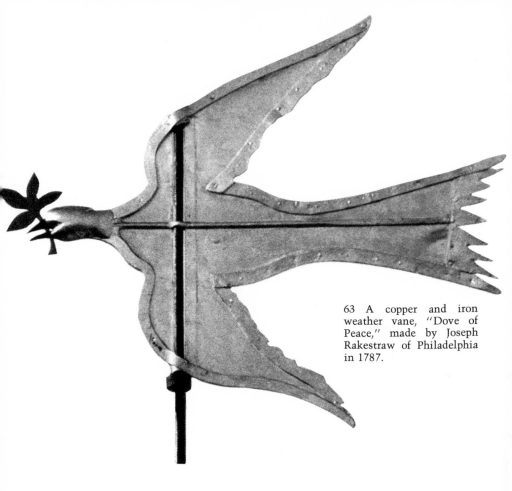

63 A copper and iron weather vane, "Dove of Peace," made by Joseph Rakestraw of Philadelphia in 1787.

cally, if not militarily, it marked an effective end to the conflict. But Washington also knew that the euphoria following Yorktown could seriously weaken the American negotiating position in Paris. If the war-weary republic fell into quarrelsome and factious infighting or if financial support for the army evaporated, the great powers would surely take advantage of the situation by carving out zones of influence in America or denying the new nation full sovereignty.

The interlude between Yorktown and the signing of the peace treaty—that is, from October 1781 to November 1783—was therefore a perilous one. Two episodes illustrated the danger. In May

155

1782 General Guy Carleton arrived in New York City to replace Clinton. Carleton had no intention of simply presiding over British evacuation. He did evacuate Savannah and Charles Town, but he wanted to increase the strength of the garrison at New York City and then use possession of that city as a negotiating pawn. In this way he hoped to persuade Congress to acknowledge that Americans were still subjects of the king. By this time, however, the British government was firmly committed to recognizing American independence, so nothing came of Carleton's scheme. But if he had been strongly supported by the new ministry, Carleton's stalling tactics and his control of a large garrison in New York City would have confronted Congress with enormous diplomatic and military difficulties.[6]

Then in December 1782 a group of impetuous American army officers stationed at Newburgh, New York, threatened to take matters into their own hands if they did not receive payment of long overdue salaries. This "Newburgh conspiracy" played directly into the hands of a clique of nationalist politicians who wanted Congress to have extensive new powers, including the power to tax and to create a large peacetime army. The possibility of a coup by disgruntled officers was just the sort of crisis needed to force Congress to seize broad new powers. When Washington heard of the officers' demands, he confronted the leaders and in an emotional speech shamed them for their disloyalty and indiscretion. The long transition from war to peace had tested and strengthened the internal cohesion of the new republic.

Notes

[1] Patrick Ferguson to General Henry Clinton, November 22, 1779, Clinton Papers, William L. Clements Library, Ann Arbor, Michigan.

[2] E. James Ferguson, *The Power of the Purse: A History of American Public Finance, 1776–1790* (Chapel Hill: University of North Carolina Press, 1961), pp. 3–69.

[3] Quoted in Piers Machesy, *The War for America, 1775–1783* (London: Longmans, Green, and Co., 1964), p. 404.

[4] Donald L. Robinson, *Slavery in the Structure of American Politics, 1765–1820* (New York: Harcourt Brace Jovanovich, 1971), p. 120.

⁵ Ronald Hoffman, *A Spirit of Dissension: Economics, Politics, and the Revolution in Maryland* (Baltimore: Johns Hopkins University Press), pp. 184–241.
⁶ Paul H. Smith, "Sir Guy Carleton, Peace Negotiations, and the Evacuation of New York," *Canadian Historical Review*, L (1969), pp. 245–64.

Bibliography

The best introductions to the study of the Revolutionary War are John Shy, "The American Revolution: The Military Conflict Considered as a Revolutionary War," in Stephen G. Kurtz and James H. Hutson, eds., *Essays on the American Revolution* (Chapel Hill: University of North Carolina Press, 1973); Don Higginbotham, *The American War for Independence: Military Attitudes, Policies, and Practice, 1763–1789* (New York: Macmillan, 1971); and John Richard Alden, *The American Revolution, 1775–1783* (New York: Harper Brothers, 1953). Exceptionally readable and original assessments of military leadership appear in George A. Billias, ed., *George Washington's Generals* and *George Washington's Opponents* (New York: William Morrow, 1964, 1969). Piers Machesy, *The War for America, 1775–1783* (London: Longmans, 1964) places the war in a global setting and focuses on the decision-making process in London. Ira D. Gruber, *The Howe Brothers and the American Revolution* (New York: Atheneum, 1972) examines the tangled political, personal, military, and social relationships between ministers and generals during the early stages of the war.

The best way to immerse oneself in the intricate details of the war is to read several of the excellent available biographies of leading generals. William B. Willcox, *Portrait of a General: Sir Henry Clinton in the War for Independence* (New York: Alfred Knopf, 1962) is the ablest of these, in part because Willcox discovered a technique for examining Clinton psychologically; see William B. Willcox and Frederick Wyatt, "Sir Henry Clinton: A Psychological Exploration in History," *WMQ*, XVI (1959), 3–26. No biography of Washington equals the penetration and acuteness of Willcox's *Clinton*, but Douglass Southall Freeman, *George Washington*, 7 vols. (New York, Scribner's, 1948–1957), and James T. Flexner, *George Washington*, 4 vols. (Boston: Little, Brown, 1965–1972) are capable, readable, and authoritative. Franklin and Mary Wickwire, *Cornwallis: The American Adventure* (Boston: Houghton Mifflin, 1970); Don Higginbotham, *Daniel Morgan: Revolutionary Rifleman* (Chapel Hill: University of North Carolina Press, 1961); Robert D. Bass, *The Green Dragoon: The Lives of Banastre Tarleton and Mary Robinson* (New York: Holt, Rinehart, and Winston, 1957); Hugh F. Rankin, *Francis Marion: The Swamp Fox* (New York: Thomas Y. Crowell, 1973); John R. Alden, *General Gage in America: Being Principally a History of his Role in the American Revolution* (Baton   157

Rouge: Louisiana State University Press, 1948), and *General Charles Lee: Traitor or Patriot?* (Baton Rouge: Louisiana State University Press, 1951) are excellent biographies.

On the role of Indians in the war, see Barbara Graymont, *The Iroquois in the American Revolution* (Syracuse: Syracuse University Press, 1972); James H. O'Donnell III, *Southern Indians in the American Revolution* (Knoxville: University of Tennessee Press, 1973); and Jack Sosin, "The Use of Indians in the War of the American Revolution: A Reassessment of Responsibility," *Canadian Historical Review*, XLVI (1965), 101–21.

On the loyalists, see William H. Nelson, *The American Tory* (Oxford: Oxford University Press, 1961), whose characterization of groups of loyalists as "cultural minorities" remains the most significant single interpretation of their place in the Revolution; Wallace Brown, *The Good Americans: The Loyalists in the American Revolution* (New York: William Morrow, 1969); Mary Beth Norton, *The British Americans: The Loyalist Exiles in England* (Boston: Little, Brown, 1972); and Robert M. Calhoon, *The Loyalists in Revolutionary America, 1760–1781* (New York: Harcourt Brace Jovanovich, 1973).

On the impact of the Revolution on American blacks, see Duncan McLeod, *Slavery, Race, and the American Revolution* (Cambridge: Cambridge University Press, 1974); Benjamin Quarles, *The Negro in the American Revolution* (Chapel Hill: University of North Carolina Press, 1961); Mary Beth Norton, "The Fate of Some Black Loyalists of the American Revolution," *Journal of Negro History*, LVIII (1973), 402–26; Arthur Zilversmit, *The First Emancipation: The Abolition of Slavery in the North* (Chicago: University of Chicago Press, 1967); and Winthrop D. Jordan, *White Over Black: American Attitudes Toward the Negro, 1550–1812* (Chapel Hill: University of North Carolina Press, 1968).

The impact of the war on American society must be pieced together from a wide variety of writings, in particular Lee Nathaniel Newcomer, *The Embattled Farmers: A Massachusetts Countryside in the American Revolution* (New York: Columbia University Press, 1954); Joel A. Cohen, "Rhode Island Loyalism and the American Revolution," *Rhode Island History*, XXVII (1968), 97–105; Gwilym Roberts, "An Unknown Vermonter: Sylvanus Ewarts . . .," *Vermont History*, XXIX (1961), 92–102; Hamilton Bail, "Zadock Wright . . .," *Vermont History*, XXXVI (1968), 186–203; Sydney V. James, *A People Among Peoples: Quaker Benevolence in Eighteenth-Century America* (Cambridge: Harvard University Press, 1963); Mack Thompson, *Moses Brown: Reluctant Reformer* (Chapel Hill: University of North Carolina Press, 1962); Leonard Lundin, *Cockpit of the Revolution: The War for Independence in New Jersey* (Princeton: Princeton University Press, 1940); Adrian C. Leiby, *The Revolutionary War in the Hackensack Valley: The Jersey Dutch and the Neutral Ground* (New

Brunswick, N. J.: Rutgers University Press, 1962); Thomas J. Wertenbaker, *Father Knickerbocker Rebels: New York City During the Revolution* (New York: Charles Scribner, 1948); Barbara Graymont, *The Iroquois in the American Revolution* (Syracuse: Syracuse University Press, 1972); Henry J. Young, "Treason and its Punishment in Revolutionary Pennsylvania," *Pennsylvania Magazine of History and Biography*, XC (1966), 278–91; Ronald Hoffman, *A Spirit of Dissension: Economics, Politics, and the Revolution in Maryland* (Baltimore: Johns Hopkins University Press, 1974); John K. Alexander, "The Fort Wilson Incident of 1779: A Case Study of the Revolutionary Crowd," *WMQ*, XXXI (1974), 589–612; Hugh F. Rankin, *The North Carolina Continentals* (Chapel Hill: University of North Carolina Press, 1971); Gary D. Olson, "Loyalists and the American Revolution: Thomas Brown and the South Carolina Backcountry, 1775–1776," *South Carolina Historical Magazine*, LXVIII (1967), 201–19 and LXIX (1968), 45–56; George Smith McCowen, *The British Occupation of Charleston, 1780–1782* (Columbia: University of South Carolina Press, 1972); Russell F. Weigley, *The Partisan War: The South Carolina Campaign of 1780–1782* (Columbia: University of South Carolina Press, 1970); Richard Maxwell Brown, "The Violent Origins of South Carolina Extremism," forthcoming; Patrick J. Furlong, "Civilian-Military Conflict and the Restoration of the Royal Province of Georgia, 1778–1782," *Journal of Southern History*, XXXVIII (1972), 415–42; and Gary D. Olson, "Thomas Brown: Loyalist Partisan and the Revolutionary War in Georgia, 1777–1782," *Georgia Historical Quarterly*, LIV (1970), 1–19, 183–207.

On the Newburgh conspiracy, see Richard H. Kohn, "The Inside History of the Newburgh Conspiracy: America and the Coup d'Etat," *WMQ*, XXVII (1970), 187–220, and Don Higginbotham, *The American War for Independence* (New York: Macmillan, 1971), pp. 405–12. On the rival military philosophies of the Continental Army and the militia, see Russell F. Weigley, *Towards an American Army* (New York: Columbia University Press, 1962).

On Revolutionary diplomacy see Felix Gilbert, *To the Farewell Address: Ideas of Early American Foreign Policy* (Princeton: Princeton University Press, 1961) and Richard B. Morris, *The Peacemakers: The Great Powers and American Independence* (New York: Harper and Row, 1965).

For an elaboration of some of the themes in this chapter, see Robert M. Calhoon, "The Floridas, the Western Frontier, and Vermont: Thoughts on the Hinterland Loyalists," in Samuel Proctor, ed., *Eighteenth-Century Florida: Life on the Frontier* (Gainesville: University Presses of Florida, 1976) and "Civil, Revolutionary, or Partisan: The Loyalists and the Nature of the War for Independence" in the *Proceedings* of the Air Force Academy Symposium on the War for Independence to be published in 1976 by the Government Printing Office.

Constitutionalism 4

It may be a reflection on human nature that such devices should be necessary to control the abuses of government. But what is government but the greatest of all reflections on human nature? If men were angels, no government would be necessary. If angels were to govern men, neither external nor internal controls on government would be necessary. In framing a government which is to be administered by men over men, the great difficulty lies in this: you must first enable the government to control the governed, and in the next place, oblige it to control itself.*

James Madison, *The Federalist*, Number 51

CONSTITUTION-MAKING AT THE STATE LEVEL

The American Revolution was the first and most successful of a long series of upheavals in the western world during the last quarter of the eighteenth century—a period properly labeled "the age of the democratic revolution." During the late eighteenth century the term "democratic" did not mean majority rule; it referred rather to a political system based on the consent of the people as

---

* Jacob E. Cooke, ed., *The Federalist* (Cleveland: World Publishing Company, 1961), p. 349.

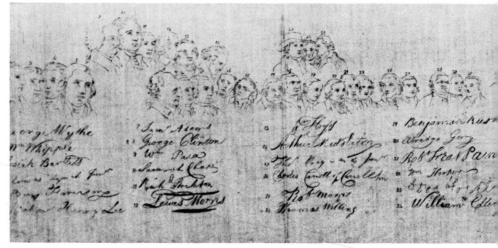

64 Print on a kerchief depicting the signing of the Declaration of Independence.

expressed through representative institutions and required that
political power not become the exclusive prerogative of particular
orders or classes of society. While the American and French revolutions were the most dramatic and far-reaching struggles of the
period, serious democratic movements also developed between
1760 and 1790 in Ireland, England, Poland, Belgium, Switzerland,
Sweden, and—in the wake of the wars of the French Revolution—in many other parts of Europe. Rooted in particular internal
causes, these movements also reflected certain underlying changes
in western society: a rapidly growing and affluent middle class; a
burgeoning world economy in which merchants, lawyers, and
other energetic professional people played an increasingly important role; and a relatively slow and incomplete advance in modern-
ization of institutions like churches, legal systems, banks, and
bureaucracies.

One manifestation of this ferment and restlessness was the belief
among economically rising and acquisitive classes that the attain-
ment and exercise of political power could and should be regulated
in the public interest through the use of reason and experience. By
reason was meant the ideas of classical, Renaissance, and Enlightenment philosophy, and by experience was meant the study of his-
162   tory. The whole pre-Revolutionary controversy had been fueled on

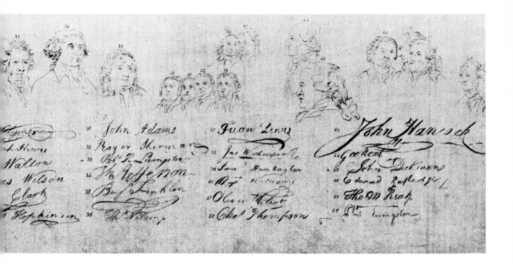

the colonial side, from 1760 to 1775, by a search for historical evidence and philosophical concepts that would enable the Americans to define liberty. This search forced people to think in constitutional terms—that is, to think of themselves as a nation of individuals drawn together by history, heritage, and association into a covenantal relationship and, for the sake of that covenant, obligated to discover the real location of power within their society and the moral rules that should govern the use of that power. "Knowing the strong bias of human nature to tyranny and despotism," the Pittsfield, Massachusetts, Town Meeting resolved on May 29, 1776, "we have nothing else . . . to provide . . . posterity against the wanton exercise of power . . . than the formation of a fundamental constitution" for the state of Massachusetts.[1]

Although constitution-making raised serious philosophical questions and summoned forth leaders of extraordinary vision and ability, it would be a mistake to see the process simply as a heroic and somewhat intellectual enterprise. Constitutions were practical tools for holding American society together and for allowing the energies released by the Revolution to be given full play. The most striking social change in Revolutionary society was the appearance of a new breed of local politicians. Some were New England privateers who got rich seizing British shipping, others were merchants 163 who profited from army contracts, and still others were obscure officials who had filled posts in local government during the war and had gained a taste for power and importance. The Revolution opened territories west of the Appalachians for settlement and speculation, initiated a flood of emigration, and created intense conflicts between rival claimants and speculators. This westward surge required the expulsion or pacification of thousands of Indians and a policy of forced treaties and military measures that insured white access to the frontier. Finally, the Revolution both called into question the legitimacy of slavery and made slave owners aware that determined political action would be needed to protect the institution of black bondage. By placing national destiny in the hands of the people, the Revolution made American society more democratic, open, and competitive, and at the same time more exploitive, unrestrained, violent, and racist. Constitutional government reinforced and perpetuated those contradictory aspects of American character.

The impetus for constitution-making sprang—like almost every other step in the American Revolution after 1774—simultaneously from the Continental Congress and from local communities. As British officials fled to the refuge of garrisons and warships, and colonial governments simply ceased to function in 1775 and early 1776, various provincial congresses asked the Continental Congress for guidance. In replies to individual colonies as early as October 1775, and in a general directive to all of the colonies the following May, Congress recommended the drafting of constitutions based on the sovereignty of the people and designed to protect their liberties. By the time independence was declared in July 1776, three states—New Hampshire, South Carolina, and Virginia—had adopted new constitutions; and by the end of the year Pennsylvania, Delaware, New Jersey, Maryland, and North Carolina had joined the list. Rhode Island and Connecticut simply removed all reference to British authority from their original colonial charters. New York, Georgia, and Vermont approved new constitutions in 1777. Massachusetts did not reach agreement on its constitution until 1780.

The effort to produce a constitution in each of the states involved two different kinds of political struggle. In almost every state there was a clash between those who were suspicious of the power of aristocrats and confident of the virtue of the people, and those who were skeptical of the virtue of the people and wished to rely on the superior wisdom of leaders of wealth and position. Several widely read pamphlets defined the issues facing the states in 1776. Paine's *Common Sense* assured Americans that they were a pure, energetic, and virtuous people uniquely equipped for self-government. *The People, the Best Governors,* an anonymous Massachusetts pamphlet, condemned all attempts to entrust power to a privileged elite, especially property qualifications for voting and a bicameral legislature. An anonymous Pennsylvania pamphlet, *Four Letters on Interesting Subjects,* feared that a rigid separation of powers and a bicameral legislature would unnecessarily divide people and intensify political conflicts. Against these democratic theorists, John Adams's *Thoughts on Government* proved to be a powerful rebuttal. Arguing for a formal separation of legislative, executive, and judicial power and a bicameral legislature, Adams stated that human passions and ambitions were so strong that a formal structure, rooted in English and colonial historical experience, was needed to inhibit and restrain individuals and groups. What was also at stake was the search for a workable and broadly acceptable means of converting the theory of popular sovereignty into functioning political practices.

The first state constitution was adopted by the Revolutionary congress in New Hampshire in January 1776; there was no special constitutional convention and no process for ratification. The constitution, an uneasy compromise between western towns and coastal Portsmouth, satisfied no one, and the state spent the years 1778 until 1784 wrangling over a revised charter of government. In March 1776 the South Carolina Provincial Congress adopted a constitution on the advice of the Continental Congress. Many legislators doubted the legitimacy of the document. A new constitution in 1778 kept power firmly in the hands of the lowland aristocracy. In May 1776 Virginia adopted a constitution, also without popular

65 An illustration from the 1771 *New England Primer* that was altered by crossing out George III's name and substituting that of George Washington.

sanction or ratification, but it carefully delineated the powers of the executive, legislative, and judicial branches of the government and contained a bill of rights protecting individual civil liberties. In New Jersey, Delaware, Pennsylvania, North Carolina, Maryland, New York, and Massachusetts, voters elected drafting conventions or provincial congresses with express authority to draft constitutions and thereby gave prior consent to the constitution-making process.

Prior public knowledge of constitution-making made the whole process more contentious, complex, and scrupulous. Delaware's constitution was the first drafted by a convention elected exclusively for that purpose; the voters elected a majority of British sympathizers, who reflected fairly accurately the loyalist views of a majority of the populace during the early years of the war. Pennsylvania's constitution was unique. The traditional Whig leaders who had organized the Revolutionary movement in the colony in 1774 and 1775 were driven from power by brash newcomers. Politically inexperienced and resentful of the predominance of the wealthy, propertied Whigs, the Pennsylvania radicals took advantage of the fierce infighting among the Penn family, the Quakers, the Presbyterians, and other groups that had plagued and divided the colony for decades. Usurping authority from the old assembly, the Pennsylvania radicals abolished the office of governor and substituted a popularly elected Executive Council of twelve members; there was no upper house but only a lower assembly. Property qualifications for voting or officeholding were replaced by a simple tax-paying requirement. Laws were to be posted for public inspection and reaction for months before they went into effect. The only checks on the behavior of government were the will of the people and the scrutiny of a Council of Censors, which would meet every seven years and review the constitutionality of legislative decisions. In contrast with Pennsylvania, North Carolina easily reconciled the views of its popular leaders in the western counties of Orange and Mechlenberg with those of its lowland aristocratic leaders; borrowing heavily from the Virginia constitution and from John Adams's *Thoughts on Government,* the North Carolina constitution acknowledged that power resides in the whole people and established a conventional separation of executive, legislative, and judicial power. The Georgia constitution allowed for amendment of its articles by a convention that could be summoned by popular petition, and the New York constitution was an uneasy compromise between hostile aristocratic and middle-class factions, which were bitterly divided over questions of taxation, militia administration, and regulation of the economy.

The most significant and protracted constitution-making occurred in Massachusetts. Faced with a restive populace and demands from western towns for radical constitutional experimentation, the legislature decided to draft its own constitution with the assurance that it would be submitted for ratification to all of the voters. Outraged by that seemingly highhanded tactic, the voters overwhelmingly rejected the constitution presented to the towns in 1778. The legislature then submitted to the demand for a special convention, which met in 1779. It produced a plan for a conventional separation of powers, graduated property qualifications for voting and officeholding—higher qualifications for voting for the senate than the lower house, and qualifications for officeholding increasing upward according to the importance of the post—and a complicated procedure for ratification in which towns voted separately on each article. Only by an involved tabulation did officials declare the document as a whole to be ratified.

These constitutions were, for several reasons, the most important achievements of the whole Revolutionary period. They gave concrete meaning to the concept of popular sovereignty. It had been an article of faith during the pre-Revolutionary controversy that the king ruled the colonies only by the implied consent of the people, as expressed in their colonial charters, and that if he grossly violated their liberties he would forfeit his legitimate authority. In that event, power would revert to the whole body of the people. When various provincial congresses found themselves in custody of rebellious colonies, that very contingency seemed to have arrived. At this first threshold of political independence, the primary concerns of Whig leaders were the maintenance of a continuity of civil authority, the legitimacy of the new provincial assemblies and governments created by state constitutions, and the security of Revolutionary regimes against British attempts to reimpose royal authority.

These concerns were, of course, closely intertwined. If law and order collapsed, some moderate people would welcome the return of British rule. Only a legitimate government—one clearly created and supported by the will of the community—would be able to mobilize and direct military resistance. If the allies of the Crown—whether labeled "Tories" or simply "persons inimical" to American liberty—were to be isolated and immobilized, then the widest degree of involvement in, and commitment to, the new government had to be achieved. A constitution would serve to dissociate the Revolution from the names of a few prominent leaders and identify it instead with the entire state and with the Continental Congress itself. Finally speed—though not haste—was necessary. In meeting these requirements, the states developed a kind of formula of Revolutionary constitution-making, a formula that became more elaborate as each state drafted its own constitution and added to the accumulation of precedent. The formula held that constitutions should be written documents, drafted in behalf of the whole people by specially summoned constitutional conventions; that constitutions should acknowledge the ultimate power of the people, should safeguard their civil liberties, should institute some scheme of representation that reflected the popular will and the special role of the elite; that there should be provision for amendment or revision of state constitutions and that there should be ratification by the people.

ORGANIZING THE POLITY

The 1780s have been called a "critical period" in the shaping of institutions and the development of political practices in the United States. It was not, however, critical in the sense that society and government were suffering from deep-rooted malaise—as nineteenth-century nationalist historians supposed. Rather it was a period of critical choices for politically conscious Americans. For as the new nation dealt with practical, immediate political

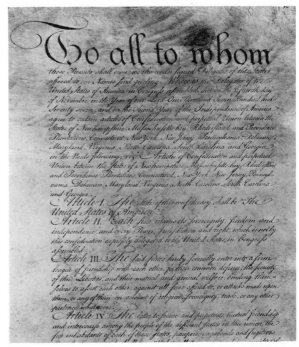

66   The first page of the Articles of Confederation.

problems, it also began to perceive the possibilities and difficulties of the future: how cohesive a political entity the United States would be, how much internal animosity the society could tolerate without damage to its own stability and health, and how the pursuit of wealth should be regulated.

The Articles of Confederation, drafted by Congress in 1776 and 1777 and not finally ratified until 1781, provided a preview of the coming struggle over the concrete meaning that would be given to concepts of republican government and national character. John Dickinson's initial draft of the Articles of Confederation simply formalized the Revolutionary institutions that had come into being since 1774. Congress would continue to have widespread authority to govern, there would be no separate executive, and states would retain the power of taxation. Even so modest a step toward the creation of a national government, however, aroused sectional and economic division and hostility that had been held in check by the more urgent tasks of declaring independence, launching state governments, and starting to fight a war. Led by Thomas Burke of North Carolina and Edward Rutledge of South Carolina, Congress inserted into the Articles an emphatic declaration that "each state retains its sovereignty, freedom, and independence." Each state had one vote based on a poll of its delegation. A majority of the thirteen states could enact routine measures, while nine states had to concur before major measures passed. Amendment of the Articles required unanimous consent. The advocates of a strong national government, however, won important concessions: the "Privileges and immunities of free citizens" of any state were extended to all free citizens; the Confederacy was responsible for its own debts; states could not conduct foreign policy and could not enter into compacts with other states without the consent of Congress; and elaborate machinery was created to resolve interstate conflicts. Thus, the first American constitution was an amalgam of state rights and nationalist principles. The balance between national and state power tilted heavily toward the sovereignty of the states, but the Articles did create a national government to replace the ad hoc machinery of the Continental Congress. Simply creating such a compromise document under the stresses of war indicated the

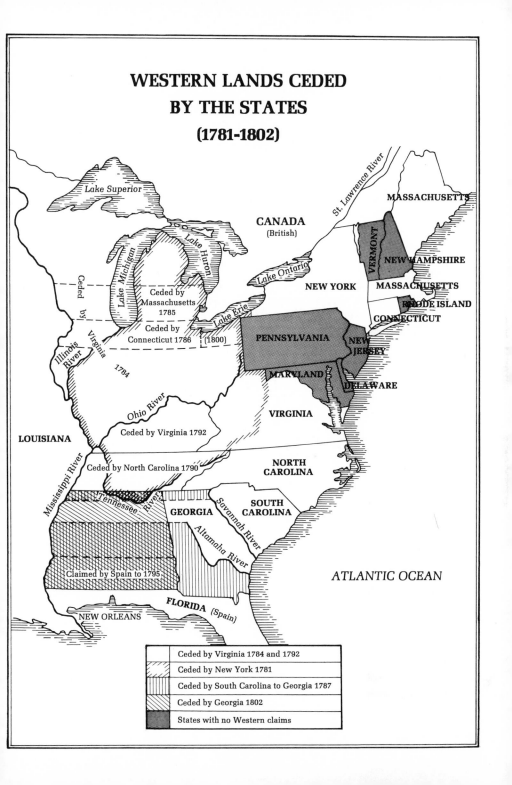

WESTERN LANDS CEDED
BY THE STATES
(1781-1802)

Lake Superior

CANADA
(British)

MASSACHUSETTS

St. Lawrence River

VERMONT

NEW HAMPSHIRE

Lake Huron

Lake Michigan

Ceded by
Massachusetts
1785

Lake Ontario

NEW YORK

MASSACHUSETTS

Ceded
by

Virginia

Lake Erie

Ceded by
Connecticut 1786 (1800)

PENNSYLVANIA

RHODE ISLAND

CONNECTICUT

NEW
JERSEY

Illinois River

1784

Ohio River

MARYLAND

DELAWARE

VIRGINIA

LOUISIANA

Ceded by Virginia 1792

Ceded by North Carolina 1790

NORTH
CAROLINA

Mississippi River

Tennessee River

GEORGIA

Savannah River

SOUTH
CAROLINA

Altamaha River

Claimed by Spain to 1795

ATLANTIC OCEAN

FLORIDA (Spain)

NEW ORLEANS

Legend	
	Ceded by Virginia 1784 and 1792
	Ceded by New York 1781
	Ceded by South Carolina to Georgia 1787
	Ceded by Georgia 1802
	States with no Western claims

capacity of the republic for national decision-making. In this sense the Articles of Confederation were a threshold on the path toward the Federal Constitution.

The major achievement of the Confederation period, a policy for administering western land, was a byproduct of the ratification process. Seven states—Massachusetts, Connecticut, New York, Virginia, North and South Carolina, and Georgia—claimed land west of the Appalachians, and the remaining states refused to ratify the Articles until these claims were relinquished. After four years of maneuver and negotiation Virginia and New York in 1781 led the way in complying with this demand. Satisfied with this degree of progress in the creation of a national domain of western land, the landless states ratified the Articles. Virginia attempted to retain control over Kentucky and furthermore demanded that Congress invalidate land sales in the Ohio Valley made by Indians to Maryland and Pennsylvania speculators. After a protracted and complex struggle, Virginia and the Continental Congress finally reached an accommodation in 1784 by which Virginia withdrew its claim to Kentucky, and Congress invalidated the claims of the northern speculators. In this way Virginia assisted Congress in finding desperately needed revenue—from land sales in the West—and protected the interests of former Virginia Revolutionary War officers who hoped to secure land in the West in payment for their services in the war.

This settlement opened the way for Congress to develop a comprehensive policy for distribution of western land and the evolution of a political system in the frontier. The Land Ordinance of

67 Cincinnati on the Ohio River in 1807.

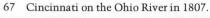

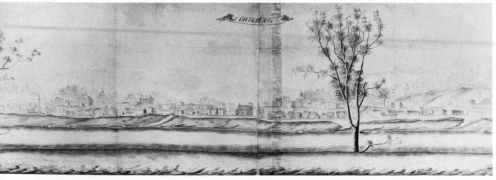

68 The future site of Cleveland, Ohio, where the Cuyahoga River enters Lake Erie, as it appeared in 1796.

1785 provided for the division of the Northwest Territory—the future states of Ohio, Indiana, Illinois, and Michigan—into townships of six square miles and those subdivided into 640-acre sections. It also allowed a high degree of local self-government. Intended to rationalize and accelerate land settlement, the ordinance created a chaotic situation. The Ohio Company of Virginia persuaded Congress to sell it six and one-half million acres, heightening rivalry with other speculator groups and giving rise to conflicts with the thousands of illegal squatters who simultaneously flooded the region. To regain some control over the situation, Congress passed in 1787 the Northwest Ordinance, which placed the region under the control of governors and other officials ap-

69 Nathan Dane of Massachusetts, a drafter of the Northwest Ordinance.

70   The Ohio Company garrison at the mouth of the Muskingum River, Ohio, in 1792.

pointed by Congress. Voting was limited to those owning at least fifty acres of land. Slavery was forbidden. The Northwest Territory could be divided into three, four, or five states. As soon as five thousand adult males settled in any portion of the region, a territorial government could be created, although the Congressionally appointed governor would have an absolute veto over the popularly elected legislature. In practice, the ordinance enabled prominent speculator families with good connections in Congress to establish themselves as a dominant elite in the western territories. Once Congress decided that a territory merited statehood, however, it would enter the Union as a full equal with the older states. The ordinance therefore established a stable political order by dividing power between aggressive land speculators and powerful Congressional factions. It provided a framework within which rapid western expansion could occur.

The price paid for rapid sale and settlement of western land was Indian removal—an example of the harsh, exploitive energies released by the American Revolution. In the Treaty of Fort Stanwix in 1784 Congressional commissioners pressured Iroquois leaders into surrendering all of their claims to land in the Northwest Territory, and the following year in the Treaty of Fort McIntosh the Chippewa, Ottawa, Delaware, and Wyandot tribes surrendered most of their claims to Northwest land. These agreements did not

174

settle matters. The tribes in the region denied that the Iroquois had any right to cede western lands to the white settlers, and the Shawnee refused to sign the Fort McIntosh agreement. As illegal squatters began to flood the contested territory, Congressional commissioners, fearful of an outbreak of fighting, finally induced the Shawnee to accept the Fort McIntosh cession in 1786. Almost at once the agreement collapsed, and by 1787 the tribes of the Northwest had repudiated all of their prior cessions of land to the American government. Not until 1794 did Indian resistance collapse under the dual blows of General Anthony Wayne's defeat of the Indians at the Battle of Fallen Timbers and the decision of the British government, overextended during the Napoleonic wars, to abandon its Northwest forts and withdraw aid to its Indian allies.

The settlement of western land policy by the Confederation Congress—which created a decentralized political order in the West dominated by well-connected insiders and nourished by rapid land speculation and Indian removal—was an important step in determining what kind of political order would emerge in the new republic. Equally important in shaping American society was the development of the state legislatures in the 1780s. In struggling with matters of taxation, land distribution, salaries of elected and appointed officials, and policies on debt and the money supply, the legislatures under the Articles learned a great deal about the possi-

71 John Cleves Symmes, of Morristown, New Jersey, was a land speculator who in 1788 purchased a million acres north of the Ohio River. This is a certificate of conveyance that he used in selling land in this region.

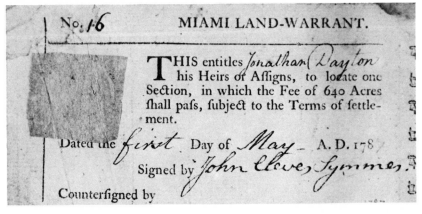

72 A Shawnee warrior in the Ohio territory.

bilities and limitations of republican government. Throughout the 1780s people looked increasingly upon the legislatures as places where clashing interests were to be reconciled and impediments to prosperity and harmony removed. While the process produced a great deal of controversy and confusion, legislative disputes were a stabilizing influence that institutionalized conflict and attracted new groups of people to politics. During the late colonial period less than one assemblyman in five could be classified as a yeoman farmer or artisan, and by the early 1780s more than 40 percent of all assembly members—and a majority of those in the northern states—were people of moderate means.

Voting on bills and resolutions tended to divide legislators into two reasonable distinct parties that Jackson T. Main, the foremost authority on state politics during the Revolution, has identified as "cosmopolitans" and "localists." Localists were those whose experience was limited to a particular locality or at least to the boundaries of their home state, while cosmopolitans through travel, education, military service, family connections, business interests, or personal friendships had frequent and well-established contacts outside their own localities and states. Localists were likely to be farmers rather than merchants, to own less property than cosmo-

73 General Anthony Wayne, victor over the Indians at the Battle of Fallen Timbers, August 20, 1794.

politans, and to live in places more remote from centers of trade. Localists tended to favor limitations on the terms of judges and government economy through lower salaries for government officials, though they understandably favored higher expense reimbursements for members of the legislatures; conversely, cosmopolitans valued judicial independence that was encouraged by a long term in office, wished to pay higher salaries to state officials, and felt less need for per diem compensation for legislators. Localists

74 Fort Wayne in the Northwest Territory in 1794.

resisted the payment of prewar debts to British creditors and were hostile to returning loyalists; cosmopolitans were more concerned with the orderly processes of law and debt recovery and preferred to absorb the former loyalists back into society. Among the leaders of each group, age and political experience were important: localists had entered politics in the 1760s and had enjoyed statewide prominence during the Revolution, while cosmopolitans had begun their careers in the 1770s and found the Continental Army and Congress the best avenues for advancement. Not surprisingly, during the controversy over ratification of the Federal Constitution, localists tended to oppose ratification, while cosmopolitans supported the new constitution.

The division between localists and cosmopolitans, between national and parochial orientations, between strong interest groups and their critics or rivals was indistinct and shifting. Conflict was not sufficiently intense to force participants toward one partisan extreme or another, and the tendency to favor compromise solutions further retarded the development of antagonistic party alignments. More than any other episode, Shays' Rebellion in Massachusetts in 1786–1787 revealed the extent and nature of economic and social conflict during the Confederation period. Farmers in western Massachusetts had, throughout the decade, resented high taxes, the requirements that taxes and many other debts be paid in silver coin, the unresponsiveness of the state senate to constituent opinion, the high cost of legal services, and the way in which lawyers in the legislature kept laws and court procedures unnecessarily complex and costly. By September 1786 discontent over these issues had reached flash point. Crowds began spontaneously occupying county courthouses and forcing judges to suspend court proceedings to prevent seizure of the lands of indebted farmers. To thwart grand jury indictment of the rioters, Daniel Shays led 1,100 men armed with clubs, who prevented the meeting of the Supreme Court on its semiannual circuit to Springfield. Most of these rioters were respectable farmers or Revolutionary War veterans— men who were deeply in debt and whose economic position had steadily deteriorated since 1781. They felt betrayed by the same republican government they had helped create.

75 and 76 Governor George Clinton, powerful New York political leader and anti-Federalist, issued this stinging proclamation denouncing Shay's Rebellion.

By HIS EXCELLENCY

George Clinton, Efq.

Governor of the STATE of NEW-YORK, General and Commander in Chief of all the Militia, and Admiral of the Navy of the fame.

A Proclamation.

WHEREAS His Excellency JAMES BOW-DOIN, anj. Governor of the Commonwealth of Maffachufetts, did iffue his proclamation, bearing date the ninth day of this inftant month of February, fetting forth, that the General Cou-t of the faid Commonwealth had, on the fourth day of the faid month declared, that a horrid and unnatural rebellion had been openly and traiteroufly, raifed and levied againft the faid Commonwealth, with defign to fubvert and overthrow the conftitution and form of governnenr thereof, and further fetting forth, that it appeared that Daniel Shays, of Pelham, and Luke Dav. of Weft Spring-

The legislature assembled almost immediately and passed three measures designed to meet the Shaysites' grievances. One law allowed payment of taxes in agricultural commodities, and another suspended legal recovery of debt for eight months. The third concession simplified court procedure in civil cases by allowing the use of court-appointed referees to resolve legal disputes before the case went to trial. These concessions did not satisfy the armed crowds, who continued their defiance, and during the winter of 1786–1787 the militia successfully dispersed them. The insurgents were poorly led and lacked organization; they had no strategy

179

beyond dramatizing their grievances. The winter that year was unusually severe. The state pardoned those who laid down their arms. Shays' followers were numerous, respectable farmers who had the capacity to bring government to a standstill; their adversaries were men of property, education, and political influence and just as much as the rioters an integral part of the social order.

The causes of Shays' Rebellion had been an inadequate money supply, arbitrary tax laws, and a cumbersome legal system. Largely these were the products of relative economic stagnation and political inexperience that the prosperity and greater political sophistication of the 1790s would alleviate. To that extent Shays' Rebellion indicated the resilience of the social order and the fact that while discontent might build, it could not renew and sustain itself. To nationalists, Shays' Rebellion was the deplorable result of inertia and drift in public affairs. The episode triggered an urgent campaign of letter-writing among nationalist critics of the Articles of Confederation throughout the country and was a grave reminder to such critics that the hour was late for the recovery of purpose and decisiveness in the affairs of the nation.

THE CONSTITUTION OF 1787

The Federal Constitution of 1787 was the final product of this long experiment in Revolutionary constitution-making. The framers adhered to the procedures established at the state level: the Constitution was drafted by a special constitutional convention, which was chosen by the representatives of the people in state legislatures and authorized by the Continental Congress; and it was ratified by popularly elected conventions. The movement to replace the Articles of Confederation with a new charter of government succeeded because a relatively small number of strategically placed men felt galled by the inability of the national government to deal with questions of finance, trade, and diplomacy. They shared a common conviction that the political development of the republic had reached a dead end. To their enemies and critics, their efforts to change the system of government appeared to be opportunistic and conspiratorial; to their nineteenth- and twentieth-century

77 The State House, Philadelphia, site of the Constitutional Convention, 1787.

admirers, they seemed destined by fate, Providence, or historical inevitability to succeed. In reality, their success demonstrated that the political order in post-Revolutionary America was highly malleable and open. The concentration of effort and will power that the nationalists brought to bear was sufficient to break through the barriers of tradition and inertia.

The chain of events leading to the drafting of the Constitution began when Congress and the states grappled with the problem of foreign trade. In 1783 the British excluded American shipping from the West Indies, and in retaliation the states—empowered by the Articles to regulate trade—placed discriminatory restrictions on British imports. But these countermeasures were too fragmented to be effective, and as a trade depression in 1784 deepened, pressure mounted to amend the Articles and permit Congress to regulate foreign trade. Eleven states agreed, but North Carolina and Rhode Island balked. Lacking unanimous support, the amendment died. The initiative lay with the advocates of constitutional change, and 181 in 1785 Maryland and Virginia arranged a conference to meet in Annapolis the following year. Though only five of the nine states that had agreed to attend actually sent delegates, the Annapolis conference had enough stature to propose a convention to meet in Philadelphia in 1787 to consider the need for constitutional reform. Mired by this time in inactivity and financial embarrassment, Congress gave the proposed meeting its official endorsement, though it authorized the delegates only to propose revisions of the Articles. Twelve states, with Rhode Island abstaining, voted to participate. Of these, eight states—Virginia, New Jersey, Pennsylvania, Delaware, Georgia, South Carolina, Connecticut, and Maryland—instructed their delegates to abide by the Annapolis conference recommendation to "render" the constitution of the nation "adequate" to its needs; New York, North Carolina, and Massachusetts authorized only revision of the Articles, and New Hampshire fell somewhere in between with its call to "remedy the defects of our federal union."

The catalyst that converted the Annapolis conference from a regional economic meeting to the convener of a constitutional convention was a diplomatic episode in 1785–1786 known as the Jay-Gardoqui negotiations. In 1784 Spain closed the mouth of the Mississippi River to American commerce. The Spanish minister to the United States, Don Diego de Gardoqui, and Congress's Secretary for Foreign Affairs, John Jay, met in New York City, under Congress's watchful eye, to resolve the impasse. Jay wanted to give up the states' navigation rights on the Mississippi in return for trade reciprocity between Spain and the United States. New England and the middle states would benefit immediately from trade with Spain, while the southern land speculators—especially in Virginia—would suffer a long-term loss in the value of their holdings from Spanish restriction of Mississippi commerce. In a vote split on sectional lines, a majority of middle and New England states instructed Jay to exchange free navigation on the Mississippi for reciprocal trade rights. The vote had no immediate practical significance, for nine states never could have been found to ratify the treaty. But the specter of a northern majority trampling on the interests of the South terrified leading Virginians. With its deep involvement in western land, the state had a strong interest in national unity. At the same time, slavery and plantation agriculture linked Virginia's interests with those of other southern states. Virginians suddenly felt in 1786 an urgent need for a national government strong enough to prevent sectional cleavage from destroying national unity. "The great danger to our national government," Madison told the Constitutional Convention, "is the great northern and southern interests being opposed to each other. Look to the votes of Congress. . . . Most of them stand divided by the geography of the country. . . ."[2]

The convention opened on May 14—though a quorum did not reach Philadelphia for another two weeks—and by August 5 the delegates had reached agreement on the essential terms of the Constitution. Several factors made that achievement possible. First, the delegates unanimously elected George Washington as presiding officer. Deliberate and dignified, Washington lacked the quick mind and political sophistication of many of the other delegates. His remoteness from the cut and thrust of debate made him an effective, trusted presiding officer. He already seemed to sense that he was a symbol of rectitude and perseverance and that his best political service to the country was the cultivation of that role. Second, the convention imposed secrecy on its deliberations: nothing that transpired could be transmitted orally or in writing to anyone outside the convention hall. The rule was never breached, even by delegates who left the meeting in disgust. This anonymity enabled the delegates to debate freely and protected the convention from becoming the focal point of a national debate during its own deliberations, which would have increased sectional rivalries within the body and inhibited the give-and-take of compromise and the ferment of tentative proposals out of which the Constitution finally evolved. A final precondition for success was the decision made on May 30 to draft a new constitution rather than simply revise the Articles. By this step the delegates defined themselves as servants of the nation with a mandate to the whole people rather than as representatives of the legislatures obligated to protect state and regional interests.

During the first three weeks of regular debate, the large-state

78 A cartoon depicting the ratification of the Constitution in Pennsylvania; the man who is leading the fight for ratification is Federalist Robert Morris.

nationalists led by James Madison of Virginia and Gouverneur Morris and James Wilson of Pennsylvania seized the initiative and won acceptance in principle for the Virginia plan. It provided for a powerful national government dominated by a bicameral legislature consisting of a lower house elected by the people and an upper house elected by the lower house from nominees proposed by the state legislatures, with representation in both houses apportioned according to population. The plan also proposed an executive and judiciary chosen by the legislature. A hastily drafted alternative New Jersey plan called for the continuation of the existing unicameral Congress, in which each state had one vote, but broadened its powers to include taxation and the regulation of trade; it also provided for a plural executive and national judiciary. But the New Jersey plan, which was favored by small-state delegates, failed to attract enough support to derail the Virginia plan. In their triumph, the nationalists, especially Madison and Wilson, misread the temper of the convention. They failed to acknowledge the deep misgivings that the small states had for the Virginia plan. At this point, in late June and early July, several new men emerged as conciliators—among them William Samuel Johnson of Connecticut and William R. Davie of North Carolina—and sought a drastic modification of the Virginia plan. By July 16 an acceptable formula was found: a bicameral legislature consisting of a lower house elected by the people with seats apportioned to states on the basis of population and an upper house with two senators from each state; five slaves counting for three whites for purposes of apportionment; exclusive power in the lower house to originate money bills; and a census every decade to readjust distribution of seats in the lower house.

This "Great Compromise" was a momentous decision. It was a finely calibrated bargain in which states and sections gained essential claims and relinquished ones that were merely desirable. A feat of political perception and imagination, it embodied two conceptions: first, a recognition that "the states . . . had never been and never would be sovereign nations and yet always had been and still meant to be discrete, self-conscious, indestructible units of political and social organization";[3] second, as William Samuel Johnson insisted, the idea that the common history of the American people had made them into "one political society."[4] Both conceptions had been around for a long time; the Great Compromise was the first successful attempt to reconcile them, to minimize the tension between them, and to exploit the ways in which indestructible states and pervasive nationalism might reinforce one another.

79 James Madison (ca. 1783), "Father of the Constitution," by Charles Willson Peale.

185

Once articulated, this juxtaposition of seemingly contrary ideas gave the embryonic Constitution a life and personality of its own. In place of wordy provisions covering every conceivable function of government, the new document became a crisp, lucid arrangement of sometimes contradictory, often contrasting, ideas about the location and use of various kinds of governmental power.

The central tension within the Constitution was its allocation of federal and state power. Unlike the Articles, in which Congress was the creature and servant of the states, and contrary to the wishes of a few extreme nationalists who wanted to submerge the states into a single national system, the Constitution provided for two nearly separate levels of governmental activity, one in the states and the other in the national government. In order to prevent conflict between the two, Congress received specific powers—among them taxation, regulation of trade, coinage of money, and defense—and broad authority to select the means by which those powers should be used. On the other hand, the states were denied specific dangerous kinds of authority such as conducting foreign policy or granting titles of nobility. Presumably the formula left the states free to handle a wide range of local problems while limiting Congress and the President to specific powerful national functions. This arrangement was designed to keep state and national government out of each other's way and hence to minimize drastically the possibilities for conflict. This delicate division of responsibility necessarily left unanswered the question of where ultimate authority rested, of how conflicts between the federal government and the states would be resolved. The Constitution hinted at the answer when it gave the Supreme Court power to enforce federal law, when it made the federal government responsible for guaranteeing a republican form of government in every state, and when it designated federal laws and treaties the "supreme law of the land."

Unlike the Confederation Congress, where each state had one vote based on a poll of individual members of state delegations, under the Constitution each representative and senator had a vote of his own. By weakening the hold of states over those members of

Congress who were inclined to act independently, the framers oriented Congress more toward the needs of the whole nation. Those provisions tilted the balance toward federal authority; but when the Bill of Rights was added as the first ten amendments to the Constitution, states' rights purists tried to regain (in the Tenth Amendment) some of this authority by specifying that all powers not expressly granted to Congress nor denied the states belonged to the states and to the people. Still, even that amendment did not say where ultimate authority rested. The controversy over slavery in the 1850s finally destroyed the vagueness about ultimate authority, as slave owners insisted that no federal law could infringe on their right to carry their property into the territories, and anti-slavery northerners demanded restrictions on the spread of slavery as a national policy. As a result, the Fourteenth Amendment enacted after the Civil War cut the heart out of the Tenth Amendment by substantially restricting the power of the states—prohibiting them from denying equal protection to any citizen. The question of ultimate authority was never again in doubt.

The mechanisms for expressing popular will about the conduct

80   Tally of votes by states in the Constitutional Convention.

New Hampshire	Massachusetts	Rhode Island	Connecticut	New York	New Jersey	Pennsylvania	Delaware	Maryland	Virginia	North Carolina	South Carolina	Georgia	Questions	ayes	noes	divided
aye	aye	no		aye	no	no	aye	aye	aye	aye			Single Executive.	7	3	
no	aye	no	aye	no	no	no	no	no	aye	no			To strike out the words "People" in the first clause of the 4th resolution; and to insert the word "Legislatures"	3	8	
no	aye	aye	no	no	no	no	aye	no	no	no			To add a convenient number of the national Judiciary to the Executive in the exercise of the negative	3	8	
aye	aye	aye	aye	aye	aye	aye	aye	aye	aye	aye			That the second Branch of the national legislature be elected by the individual legislatures.	11		
aye	no	no	no	aye	no	no	aye	no	no				To vest the national legislature with a negative on all state laws which shall appear to them improper	3	7	1
aye	no	aye	aye	aye	aye	aye	no	aye	aye				To reconsider the mode of appointing the Executive	9	2	
no	no	no	no	no	no	no	no	no	no	no			To appoint the national Executive by the Executives of the several States		10	1
aye		aye	no	no	aye	no	no	aye	aye	aye	aye		That the right of suffrage in the first branch of the national legislature ought not to be according to the rule established but according to an equitable ratio	7	3	
aye	aye	aye	no	aye	no	aye	aye	aye	aye				That the right of suffrage in the first branch be according to the whole number of white and three fifths of other inhabitants	9	2	
no	aye	aye	aye	no	aye	aye	no	no	no	no			That in the second branch of the national legislature each State have one vote	5	6	
aye	no	no	no	aye	no	no	aye	aye	aye	aye			That the right of suffrage in the second branch ought to be according to the rule established for the first an equitable rule of representation	6	5	

of government were another adroit, intricate arrangement that the framers hoped would regulate and channel political competition in the new republic. Each branch and sub-branch of government was to be chosen in a different way: the House of Representatives by all voters qualified to elect members to the lower house of their state legislature; the Senate by the state legislatures; the executive officers of the executive branch and the justices of the Supreme Court by the President with confirmation by the Senate; the President and Vice President by an electoral college chosen by the people. Reinforcing this pattern of variable modes of election and appointment were overlapping and dissimilar terms of office: the President for four years, the House for two years, the Senate for six years with one-third of the terms expiring every two years, and the Supreme Court for life. It was clearly the intention of the framers that the political and personal stakes would shift with each election. Each segment of government would be responsible to a different constituency, and each election or appointment would be the result of different interests and conditions. If corruption or irrationality occurred at one point in the electoral system, the disorder would not spread.

For the most part this design worked as intended: it postponed for at least a generation the development of a democratic political system in which Presidents and senators were as susceptible as representatives to public opinion, and yet it made certain that everyone in government held power at least indirectly by the will of the people. The flaw in the system was the electoral college, which provided that the person receiving the highest number of votes would become President and the runner-up would become Vice President. As soon as parties began to select candidates for both positions, it became necessary for a few electors to remember to throw away one of their two votes so that their party's vice-presidential candidate would come in second. When the election of 1800 ended in a tie between presidential candidate Thomas Jefferson and his running mate Aaron Burr, the Constitution had to be amended so that electors would vote for a single two-candidate slate. As a result, the section of the Constitution dealing with the election of the President and Vice President became still more complicated and cumbersome in marked contrast with the simplicity of the rest of the document. But in 1787 the convention did not anticipate any problem in the election of a President and Vice President. The establishment of the electoral college was among the last tasks of the weary delegates, who felt confident that George Washington would be elected the first chief executive and that his election would set a pattern in which two wise and respected men would naturally be elevated in a dignified manner to the two highest offices of the land.

The institution of slavery was the most divisive force within the republic, and in dealing with it the framers of the Constitution constructed another fragile compromise between the need for national unity and the strong sectional animosities that slavery had already begun to foment. The southern states, particularly South Carolina, extracted three concessions that Charles Pinckney, a South Carolina delegate to the convention, rightly boasted were, "considering all the circumstances . . . the best terms for the security of this species of property [slaves] as was in our power to make." While Congress received power to regulate foreign trade, it was forbidden for twenty years, that is, until 1808, from using that power to halt the importation of slaves. Slaves, moreover, were to count as three-fifths of white citizens for purposes of apportionment of the House of Representatives, thus, in effect, giving the slaveholding states a higher degree of representation than nonslaveholding states. Finally, runaway slaves were subject to be returned to their masters. The framers were convinced that these terms were the necessary price for southern acceptance of the Constitution. They did not doubt that slaves were property or that the protection of property rights was among the highest purposes of constitutional government. They may well have believed that the twenty-year limit on slave importation, coupled with the recent exclusion of slavery from the Northwest Territory, placed slavery at such a disadvantage that it would eventually wither and die. The Constitution was not an intentional convenant with slavery, but accommodation with slavery was one of the crucial compromises that made acceptance of the Constitution possible. In return for the three-fifths clause the northern delegates, who expected their region's population to grow faster than the South's, secured an automatic reapportionment of seats in the House every ten years instead of simply leaving reapportionment to the discretion of Congress. And the 1808 clause was part of a package favored by New England and the Deep South by which the slave states allowed Congress to tax imported slaves at ten dollars per head—insuring that the South would share equally with commercial New England the burden of import taxation. The South also agreed that direct federal taxes would be levied "in proportion" to population, thus requiring the slave owner to pay a maximum share of such a tax burden. Finally, Congress was forbidden to tax exports, a burden that would fall most heavily on the cotton-producing South and the shipping industries of New England. Thus the framers prevented slavery from disrupting the paramount task of constitution-making and used the specific interests of slave and nonslave sections of the economy as material for an intricate set of compromises.

A concluding bit of fine-tuning of the Constitution occurred when the delegates dispatched their final resolutions to a committee on style, which, Samuel E. Morison observes, "polished up the language" and in the process "rubbed out a few little things its chairman [Gouverneur Morris] did not like."[5] For example, it changed the opening words of the preamble from "We the States" to "We the People." This change was more than a literary one; it confirmed the decision made almost offhandedly at the start of the convention that the delegates would regard themselves as servants of the nation rather than as agents of the state legislatures that elected them. Further, the committee on style added an additional prohibition on the states, proscribing state laws that impaired the obligation of contract—a clause that until the twentieth century inhibited the states from regulating business enterprise.

The ratification of the Constitution by the states was a triumph of mature political deliberation. The opponents of the Constitution, called anti-Federalists, represented a broad spectrum of

BICKERSTAFF's BOSTON ALMANACK, OR, THE FEDERAL CALENDAR, For the Year of our REDEMPTION, 1788. Being Bissextile, or Leap-Year, and Twelfth of INDEPENDENCY.

Reprefentation of the FEDERAL CHARIOT.

[See the Explanation, in the next Page.]

THIRD EDITION.

Sold by E. RUSSELL, at his Office next Liberty-Pole.

81   Thirteen freemen pull Washington and Franklin toward ratification of the Constitution and the "redemption" of the country in the twelfth year of its independence.

opinion that was fearful of the role of privilege and money in politics; they were usually people whose political experience was limited to local and state affairs and who resented the prospect of a new political order that would undermine their prominence. The advocates of ratification, the Federalists, were on the whole younger people, ambitious for prominence and power on the national level and disposed by temperament and intellect to admire the sophistication and ingenuity of the Constitution.

The Constitution won quick approval in ratification conventions in Delaware, Pennsylvania, Connecticut, Georgia, and New Jersey in December 1787 and early January 1788 because in those states the Federalists outmaneuvered their critics before the anti-Federalists could organize effective opposition. The first major tests came in Massachusetts, where more than half of the 350 delegates sent to the state convention initially opposed ratification, and in New Hampshire, where a majority of the delegates were bound by voters' instructions to vote against the Constitution. By allowing the opposition full opportunity for debate and by agreeing

191

to attach to ratification certain recommendations for amendments to the Constitution, the Massachusetts Federalists converted enough delegates to secure on February 6, 1788, a 187 to 168 vote in favor of ratification. The New Hampshire convention adjourned in February 1788 without voting, and when it reassembled in June the example of Massachusetts' ratification prompted the convention to follow suit. In Maryland and South Carolina, in April and May, Federalist leadership outargued their opponents and secured lopsided endorsement of the Constitution. Thus when the Virginia convention assembled on June 2, 1788, eight states had ratified the Constitution and a ninth affirmative vote in New Hampshire would occur before the Virginia delegates voted. Hoping to create a momentum for ratification, the framers had provided that approval of nine states would be sufficient to bring the Constitution into effect. Without Virginia, however, the new government could not have worked. Led by Patrick Henry, the best rough-and-tumble orator of his time, and the scholarly, conscientious George Mason,

82 and 83   George Mason (*above*) and Patrick Henry (*right*), leaders of the anti-Federalists in Virginia.

The Picture Exhibition.

UNION:
Or, the Twelve
Federal Pillars.

84   Because Rhode Island did not ratify the Constitution until May 29, 1790, this children's primer (ca. early 1790) mentioned only twelve states.

the Virginia anti-Federalists subjected the Constitution to an exhaustive, withering search for hidden flaws and dangers. James Madison's astute rebuttals and the stature and reputation of other leading Virginia supporters of ratification carried the day by a vote of 89 to 79. Finally, in New York powerful upstate political leaders opposed to ratification delayed the opening of a convention until mid-June. When it did meet, only 19 of the 65 delegates were pledged to vote for ratification. The threat that New York City—whose merchants believed that the Constitution would foster overseas trade—might secede from the rest of the state helped convince the delegates to approve the document by a three-vote margin. Only North Carolina and Rhode Island withheld approval and, thus isolated, had to reverse themselves and join the federation after the Constitution had already gone into operation.

CONSTITUTIONALISM AND THE PROBLEM OF AUTHORITY IN REVOLUTIONARY AMERICA

From the 1760s to the 1780s Americans stood near the conclusion of the early modern period of western history. It was a period that had begun in western Europe with the Renaissance and Reformation. That pair of intellectual and religious revolutions had shattered the unity of Christian Europe, created a new sense of individualism, and prepared the way for England, Spain, France, and the Dutch Republic to emerge as powerful, expansive, self-confident nations. That expansiveness, in turn, led to overseas exploration and colonization that pumped new wealth into the European econ-

193

omies; it also created virulent inflation that wiped out much of the power of the landed aristocracies. In the ensuing scramble for power during the sixteenth and seventeenth centuries, monarchs, aristocrats, merchants, lawyers, clergymen, and ordinary people of all kinds became transfixed with the need to gain some security. In England that struggle took the form of a series of constitutional conflicts throughout the seventeenth century, testing whether Parliament or the Crown would be supreme and whether the predominant religion of the country would be Catholic, Anglican, or Calvinist. After achieving Parliamentary supremacy, Protestant succession to the throne, and toleration for dissenters by the start of the eighteenth century, and uniting England and Scotland into one kingdom in 1707, Britain could then concentrate on establishing commercial power, internal security, and ascendency over France. These mundane eighteenth-century preoccupations seemed to mark a retreat from ideology, from the supercharged seventeenth-century preoccupation with authority and power. But the eighteenth century was no less ideological than its predecessor. In Britain and America the Country ideology and Scottish Common Sense philosophy provided an elaborate but usable set of guidelines about the nature of power and the needs of society.

All of this history was as accessible to the people of the Revolutionary generation as their bookshelf, their newspapers, or their church pew. American writers, preachers, and politicians drew confidently on the enormous, eclectic, and often contradictory body of historical experience that had accumulated during the preceding three and a half centuries. At the center of this intellectual consciousness was an abiding concern with human nature. Human beings were known to be thoroughly grasping, egocentric, capricious, and self-deluding. Piety, social duty, or intellect could curb and restrain these innate tendencies, but those civilizing influences could never alter the basic nature of humanity. The political implications of this secularized Calvinism were enormous. When the colonists perceived that British ministers and their colonial lackeys had been lured by greed and depravity into a vile conspiracy to destroy American liberty, they became irrevocably radicalized and alienated from British rule. Furthermore, the whole rationale for vesting ultimate residual authority in the whole body of the people was the expectation that stable, healthy communities were less likely to exhibit human depravity than were individual members of society.

The ratification controversy was, in the final analysis, a dispute between two conflicting interpretations of this Revolutionary view of human nature. The anti-Federalists—men who had often been localists in the politics of the 1770s and early 1780s and whose ambitions were satisfied within the system laid down by the Articles of Confederation—leveled two fundamental moral criticisms against the proposed Constitution. First, they feared that a strong and elaborate national government would encourage the growth of factions, that is, little secretive cliques seeking to influence government policy for selfish reasons of their own. Second, the anti-Federalists warned that the Constitution would place more power and temptation in the hands of federal officeholders than human nature could withstand. In this way the ideology of the Revolution became a powerful source of arguments against ratification of the Constitution.

Madison's contributions to *The Federalist* papers, a series of newspaper articles, took up this challenge and demonstrated that a Calvinist view of human nature could be used, not in the defensive manner of the anti-Federalists, but rather as a key to open new kinds of understanding, as a point of departure rather than as a settled conclusion. Factions indeed reflected humanity's grasping and conspiratorial proclivities, Madison readily conceded, but the very persistence of factions in history suggested that factional behavior was not only rooted in human nature but also in the needs of society. To deal with so complex a problem, Madison insisted, required mobilizing all of the available historical knowledge. Using examples from classical, Renaissance, Dutch, and British sources, Madison constructed a theory of factional behavior that transcended the conventional wisdom about the perniciousness of faction. Factions became less grasping, dangerous, or corrupt when government responded to their legitimate grievances. When the

For the Independent Journal.

The F Œ D E R A L I S T. No. I.

To the People of the State of New-York.

AFTER an unequivocal experience of the inefficacy of the subsisting Fœderal Government, you are called upon to deliberate on a new Constitution for the United States of America. The subject speaks its own importance; comprehending in its consequences, nothing less than the existence of the UNION, the safety and welfare of the parts of which it is composed, the fate of an empire, in many respects, the most interesting in the world. It has been frequently remarked, that it seems to have been reserved to the people of this country, by their conduct and example, to decide the important question, whether societies of men are really capable or not, of establishing good government from reflection and choice, or whether they are forever destined to depend, for their political constitutions, on accident and force. If there be any truth in the remark, the crisis, at which we are arrived, may with propriety be regarded as the æra in which that decision is to be made; and a wrong election of the part we shall act, may, in this view, deserve to be considered as the general misfortune of mankind.

This idea will add the inducements of philanthropy to those of patriotism to heighten the sollicitude, which all considerate and good men must feel for the event. Happy will it be if our choice should be decided by a judicious estimate of our true interests, unperplexed and unbiassed by considerations not connected with the public good. But this is a thing more ardently to be wished, than seriously to be expected. The plan offered to our deliberations, affects too many particular interests, innovates upon too many local institutions, not to involve in its discussion a variety

85 An excerpt from the first issue of *The Federalist*, October, 1787.

members of government represented the widest spectrum of backgrounds, interests, and regions, public officials were least vulnerable to intimidation or temptation. The Constitution was designed to encourage and institutionalize this relationship between interest groups and government. A three-way separation of powers provided interest groups with a variety of pressure points, while it also insured that favors granted by one branch would be subject to review at other levels of government. Most important, the specific powers of Congress and the wide administrative authority of the President meant that the federal government would possess sufficient authority to bestow a wide range and variety of favors on supplicant interest groups. By helping broadly based, constructive factions, and rebuffing narrow and greedy ones, government under the proposed Constitution could become a civilizing agency that would encourage groups of politicians and lobbyists to choose enlightened self-interest over crude acquisitiveness.

Madison's theory of faction was an uncanny forecast of the kind of political order that would emerge in the United States during the nineteenth century, but it would have been a weak, speculative argument on behalf of ratification if he had not also dealt with the other tenet of anti-Federalism—that human beings could not handle the amount of power that the Constitution would bestow on federal officeholders. Madison had the advantage of a superior education, and for his attack on the problem of human nature and politics he tapped the most advanced Enlightenment knowledge about the operation of the human mind and personality, which appeared in the writings of the Scottish moral philosophers. Again, Madison willingly conceded that greed and dominion were the characteristic vices of powerful political leaders; greed spawned corruption, and lust for dominion or control over other people was the essence of tyranny. As powerful and detestable as those drives might be, Madison argued, there were two other human desires that, under proper circumstances, could be still stronger. These were the desires for emulation and fame. More than wealth or dominion, human beings wanted to know they were models for others in society, that children were admonished to study and inculcate their virtues. Emulation was the opposite of popularity, for while popularity was based on stylish, transient, and superficial qualities, emulation occurred only when leaders refused to curry favor and when they willingly accepted undeserved censure in order to be true to their principles. Fame—meaning historic reputation—was still different in other ways. Politicians were acutely aware that future generations of students of history would scrutinize their public conduct. The desire to play to the demanding audience of future generations of historians represented, in Madison's view, an excellent strategic device with which to temper human nature.

The whole genius of the Constitution, Madison argued, was that it gratified the desires for both emulation and fame while at the

197

same time guarding against corruption and tyranny. The Constitution did so in a number of ways. It created a powerful President and allowed for the construction of energetic governmental departments whose members would have enough prominence, scope, and responsibility to make a record that could be examined for its public spiritedness, its sophistication, its adherence to an intelligible policy, and its intrinsic humanity. By devising different modes of election or selection for House, Senate, President, executive officials, and judges, the Constitution would place people seeking political offices on a variety of public stages, seen by somewhat different audiences, and subject to varying standards of review, criticism, and reward.

Most of all, the Constitution would rely on human nature itself to regulate the moral tone of government. "The great security against a gradual concentration of powers in the same department," Madison wrote, "consists in giving to those who admin-

86   Celebration of the ratification of the Constitution in New York City in 1788.

ister each department the necessary constitutional means and personal motives to resist encroachments of . . . others. . . . *Ambition must be made to counteract ambition.*"[6] Thus in the Watergate scandal, it was not the innate goodness of John Dean, John Sirica, Vernon Walters, Archibald Cox, or Elliot Richardson that led them to expose wrongdoing; it was rather their instinct for professional survival and their ambition to achieve success and avoid failure that prompted them to take the risky steps that led to the President's downfall. The Constitution worked in 1973–1974 exactly as Madison intended that it should work.

Madison had derived from the turbulent history of the Revolutionary era a realistic and unsentimental understanding of human nature and behavior. He knew that Americans were greedy, shortsighted, egotistical, and cantankerous; but he also believed that the western intellectual traditions—which the Revolution had forced Americans to study and embrace—held the key to modifying human behavior and subduing people's antisocial tendencies. The Revolutionary experience served that purpose because it injected a high degree of self-consciousness into political affairs and motivated people to share in the common task of locating and using power. In the process they significantly changed the tradition they had received. They had started with a belief that power lay in the whole body of the people, that virtue was attainable by those who were already economically secure and socially respected, and that liberty meant freedom from compulsion and autonomy in the pursuit of private gain. By 1788 these concepts had undergone limited but significant changes of tone and emphasis. The people were not a single, mystical entity but a collection of individuals; virtue was not a precarious victory of judgment over desire but was rather manifested in the intelligence, skill, and luck with which groups of citizens pursued common social goals; liberty, far from making a free people happy, imposed a heavy burden of duty, anxiety, and uncertainty.

The Constitution expressed, better than any other single document, what Americans had learned and exhibited about themselves during the Revolutionary era. In the 1760s the colonies were an incomplete society—economically buoyant, socially stable, politically inexperienced, lacking an intrinsic set of standards and goals—indeed, lacking a national consciousness and self-confidence. The movement to resist British measures laid the ideological basis for collective action, and the struggle for independence gave Americans the actual experience of acting as a free people. The conduct of government at the national and state levels created new institutions that were manifestly authentic and legitimate. The resulting sense of social and political competence itself became a new reservoir of energy. Seeking to preserve the legacy of the Revolution in the years after 1789, Americans formed rival political parties—Federalists and Republicans—which battled fiercely to keep foreign and fiscal policy out of the hands of those who would betray the spirit of the Revolution.

Considered as a gathering, focusing, and deployment of human energy—as a thrusting out of fears and inhibitions and a reaching forward toward a freer, more democratic, more plentiful future—the American Revolution vitiated the sense of community, social and political deference, and intricate social hierarchy that had been the hallmarks of life in the individual colonies. Thus conceived, the Revolution created an appetite for a new culture of emotionalism, human goodness and potentiality, flamboyance, and virility, which would take hold of American society in the decades to come.

Notes

[1] Oscar and Mary Handlin, eds., *The Popular Sources of Political Authority: Documents on the Massachusetts Constitution of 1780* (Cambridge: Harvard University Press, 1966), p. 91.
[2] H. James Henderson, *Party Politics in the Continental Congress* (New York: McGraw-Hill, 1974), pp. 394–99, 416.
[3] Clinton Rossiter, *1787: The Grand Convention* (New York: Macmillan, 1965), p. 193.
[4] Quoted in *ibid.*
[5] Henry Steele Commager and Samuel Eliot Morison, *The Growth of the American Republic* (New York: Oxford University Press, 1930), I, 285.
[6] Cooke, p. 349, italics added.

Bibliography

The major works on constitutionalism in Revolutionary America are
Robert R. Palmer, *The Age of the Democratic Revolution: The Challenge*

(Princeton: Princeton University Press, 1959); Gordon S. Wood, *The Creation of the American Republic, 1776–1787* (Chapel Hill: University of North Carolina Press, 1969); and J. R. Pole, *Political Representation in England and the Origins of the American Republic* (London: Macmillan, 1966).

The process of constitution-making in the states may be followed in Elisha P. Douglass, *Rebels and Democrats: The Struggle for Equal Political Rights and Majority Rule During the American Revolution* (Chapel Hill: University of North Carolina Press, 1955); Robert J. Taylor, ed., *Massachusetts, Colony to Commonwealth: Documents on the Formation of its Constitution, 1775–1780* (Chapel Hill: University of North Carolina Press, 1961); Oscar and Mary Handlin, eds., *The Popular Sources of Political Authority: Documents on the Massachusetts Constitution of 1780* (Cambridge: Harvard University Press, 1966); John P. Selsam, *The Pennsylvania Constitution of 1776* (Philadelphia: University of Pennsylvania Press, 1936); Robert L. Ganyard, "Radicals and Conservatives in Revolutionary North Carolina: A Point at Issue, the October Election, 1776," *WMQ*, XXIV (1967), 568–87; and Thad W. Tate, "The Social Contract in America, 1774–1787: Revolutionary Theory as a Conservative Instrument," *WMQ*, XXII (1965), 375–91.

On the politics of the 1780s, see H. James Henderson, *Party Politics in the Continental Congress* (New York: McGraw-Hill, 1974) and "The Structure of Politics in the Continental Congress," in Stephen G. Kurtz and James H. Hutson, eds., *Essays on the American Revolution* (Chapel Hill: University of North Carolina Press, 1973); Merrill Jensen, *The Articles of Confederation: An Interpretation of the Social-Constitutional History of the American Revolution, 1774–1789* (Madison: University of Wisconsin Press, 1940) and *The New Nation: A History of the United States During the Confederation, 1781–1789* (New York: Random House, 1950); Jackson Turner Main, *Political Parties Before the Constitution* (Chapel Hill: University of North Carolina Press, 1972) and "Government by the People: The American Revolution and the Democratization of the Legislatures," *WMQ*, XXVIII (1966), 391–407.

On Indian policy in the 1780s, see Ray Allen Billington, *Westward Expansion: A History of the American Frontier* (New York: Macmillan, 1949, 4th ed., 1974), ch. 11 and Francis S. Philbrick, *The Rise of the West, 1754–1830* (New York: Harper and Row, 1965), ch. 6.

On the drafting and ratification of the Federal Constitution, see Clinton Rossiter, *1787: The Grand Convention* (New York: Macmillan, 1965); John P. Roche, "The Founding Fathers: A Reform Caucus in Action," *American Political Science Review*, LV (1961), 799–816; Donald L. Robinson, *Slavery in the Structure of American Politics, 1765–1820* (New York: Harcourt Brace Jovanovich, 1971); Staughton Lynd, "The Compromise of 1787," in *Class Conflict, Slavery, and the United States Constitu-*

tion (Indianapolis: Bobbs Merrill, 1967), pp. 185–213; Howard A. Ohline, "Republicanism and Slavery: Origins of the Three-fifths Clause in the United States Constitution," *WMQ,* XXVIII (1971), 563–84; Robert A. Rutland, *The Ordeal of the Constitution: The Anti-Federalists and the Ratification Struggle of 1787–1788* (Norman: University of Oklahoma Press, 1966); Jackson Turner Main, *The Anti-Federalists: Critics of the Constitution, 1781–1788* (Chapel Hill: University of North Carolina Press, 1961); and Forrest MacDonald, *We the People: The Economic Origins of the Constitution* (Chicago: University of Chicago Press, 1958).

On James Madison as a constitutionalist, see Trevor Colbourn, ed., *Fame and the Founding Fathers: Essays by Douglass Adair* (New York: W. W. Norton, 1974), chs. 1–4, and Arthur O. Lovejoy, *Reflections on Human Nature* (Baltimore: Johns Hopkins University Press, 1961), pp. 47–65.

General Bibliography

The best brief histories of the Revolutionary period are Edmund S. Morgan, *The Birth of the Republic, 1763–1789* (Chicago: University of Chicago Press, 1956), and E. James Ferguson, *The American Revolution: A General History, 1760–1790* (Homewood, Ill.: Dorsey Press, 1974).

Among the books that place the Revolution in a broader historical perspective, the most successful are Richard B. Morris, *The Emerging Nations and the American Revolution* (New York: Harper and Row, 1970); Hannah Arendt, *On Revolution* (New York: Viking Press, 1963); Seymour M. Lipset, *The First New Nation: The United States in Historical and Comparative Perspective* (New York: Basic Books, 1963); Clinton Rossiter, *The American Quest, 1790–1860: An Emerging Nation in Search of Identity, Unity, and Modernity* (New York: Harcourt Brace Jovanovich, 1970); Daniel J. Boorstin, *The Americans: The Colonial Experience* and *The Americans: The National Experience* (New York: Random House, 1958, 1965); and Rowland Berthoff and John M. Murrin, "Feudalism, Communalism, and the Yeoman Freeholder: The American Revolution Considered as a Social Accident," in Stephen G. Kurtz and James H. Hutson, eds., *Essays on the American Revolution* (Chapel Hill: University of North Carolina Press, 1973).

There is an abundance of published primary sources on the Revolution. The best edited of these include Jack P. Greene, ed., *Colonies to Nation, 1763–1789* (New York: McGraw-Hill, 1967); Merrill Jensen, ed., *English Historical Documents. American Colonial Documents to 1776* (London: Eyre and Spottiswoode, 1955); Gordon S. Wood, ed., *The Rising Glory of America, 1760–1820* (New York: George Braziller, 1971); and Bernard Bailyn, ed., *The Pamphlets of the American Revolution, 1750–1776,* published to date Vol. I, *1750–1765* (Cambridge: Harvard University Press, 1965).

PHOTO CREDITS

205

Index

A 6
B 7
C 8
D 9
E 0
F 1
G 2
H 3
I 4
J 5